44 Ways to Expand the Financial Base of Your Congregation

44 Ways to Expand the Financial Base of Your Congregation

Lyle E. Schaller

Illustrated by
Edward Lee Tucker

Abingdon Press
Nashville

44 WAYS TO EXPAND THE FINANCIAL BASE
OF YOUR CONGREGATION

Copyright © 1989 by Abingdon Press

This book is printed on recycled acid-free paper.

Library of Congress Cataloging-in-Publication Data

SCHALLER, LYLE E.
   44 ways to expand the financial base of your congregation / Lyle E.
Schaller; illustrated by Edward Lee Tucker.
      p.   cm.—(Friar Tuck series)

ISBN 0-687-13286-X (alk. paper)

1. Church finance. 2. Church giving. 3. Stewardship, Christian.
I. Title. II. Title: Forty-four ways to expand the financial base of
your congregation. III. Series.
BV770.S315   1989
254.8—dc19   88-22640

95 96 97 98 99 00 01 02 03 — 15 14 13 12 11 10 9

TO
N. Vernon Blankenship
Raymond E. Brown
Roland H. Sheafor
Harold R. Watkins
and to
Bill and Bob Tucker

Contents

Foreword

Why should we ask people to give to God's work to and through the church? Why should ministers and committees of volunteers spend so much time and energy coaxing and begging people to contribute to the church? Why make all that effort?

When all is said and done, there are only two good reasons why anyone should be asked to contribute money to the church. The first is to help promote the giver's spiritual growth. When people give because they feel good about what they are supporting, they will have a sense of God's grace growing within them. The second reason is even simpler. Christian discipleship is Christian stewardship. How could it be anything else? How else do God's people grow in grace?

This book is not about *why* Christians should and do contribute to advancing God's work. This book is about *how* to ask your members to support the ministry and outreach of your church. This is not a *why* book on stewardship. It is a *how* book on encouraging people to be more generous in underwriting the costs of ministry for your congregation.

One reason this may be useful is because the task of educating your people about the ministry and outreach of your church is never finished. Every congregation represents a passing parade of God's children. Some parades include more people than others, and in some parades the movement of people in and out occurs at a faster pace, but every congregation is a passing parade of people.

The first step in looking at that *how* question is to examine the assumptions on which the financial program of your congregation is based. The first chapter of this book discusses ten of those fundamental assumptions. Your assumptions will determine much about how your leaders ask your people to contribute to your church.

A never-ending responsibility of the leaders of every Christian congregation is to teach the concept of stewardship to the members of that passing parade. The second chapter suggests several methods of doing this, beginning with young children.

The teaching of stewardship to a passing parade of members, especially if one begins with three-year-olds, rarely has the immediate effect of doubling or tripling the level of member giving. What does one do while waiting to reap the long-term benefits of that long-term stewardship education effort? One possibility is to launch a major financial appeal now. Three ways how that can be done are described in chapter 3.

For those who are not prepared to undertake one of those major appeals, it may be useful to examine the possibilities of one or more minor appeals. Eleven alternatives are offered in chapter 4.

Many of the people in that passing parade have accumulated a remarkably large share of the world's goods during their pilgrimage here on earth. A growing number are leaving part or all of what remains when they die to their church. Some of their survivors are able and willing to make generous gifts in the form of memorials. Some of the reasons behind this and suggestions on how to respond are offered in chapter 5.

The fastest growing source of income to the churches

during the 1980s has been user fees. This also has turned out to be a far more complex subject than was anticipated and is discussed in chapter 6.

The Lord loves a cheerful giver and most of the people on a local church's finance committee want choices in how to increase the number of cheerful givers. One alternative is to focus on teaching stewardship as suggested in the second chapter. Seventeen additional alternatives are offered in the next three chapters. For those not satisfied with seventeen choices, another twenty-six are offered in chapter 7.

Obviously no one congregation is prepared to implement all of the forty-four ways to expand the financial base offered in this book. For some a comprehensive stewardship education program is the logical next step. Others will want to choose from among the other forty-three choices. Suggestions for next steps are offered in a brief final chapter.

The primary purposes of this book are to focus on the *how*, not the *why*, and to offer choices. Take your choice!

In offering choices to your people you may decide it would be helpful to reproduce some of the cartoons in this book. Individuals purchasing this book are hereby granted permission to reproduce these cartoons in local church publications or for use in presentations at congregational meetings. Invite Friar Tuck to help you communicate the message of this book to your people!

CHAPTER ONE

What Are Your Assumptions?

"The missions committee wants permission from this board to schedule a special appeal for the second Sunday in March," announced Hank Powell who chaired the committee. "We hope to raise at least $2,500 extra for the relief of hunger in various parts of the world. This would be in addition to what we have in the budget for missions."

"That's a worthy cause, and I would like to support your request, but three years ago we adopted a rule limiting the number of special appeals to six per year, and we already have approved six for this fiscal year," cautioned Pat Harrison who chaired the meeting.

It was the September meeting of the governing board at First Church. The twelve-member board consisted of the pastor, the treasurer, the secretary, the president of the congregation, who also chaired the board, and one person from each of the eight standing committees at First Church. The president, secretary, and treasurer were elected each year at the annual meeting in January and each committee chose its own representative to the board. In most, but not all, cases, this was the person who chaired that committee.

Proponents of this system contend it reinforces the internal communication and reporting systems, facilitates coordination, strengthens the committee structure, improves accountability, reduces conflict, and centralizes administration.

The opponents argue it places too much authority in the hands of a few, reduces participation, produces an elite leadership cadre, overloads a few people, leaves most members feeling powerless, unnecessarily limits the authority of the committees since most committee decisions have to be ratified at the monthly board meeting, and undermines the authority and leadership role of the pastor.

Others recognize the perfect system does not exist, every structure for congregational governance requires tradeoffs and conclude there are more important issues to worry about in today's world.

"I have no objection to raising more money for missions," declared Terry Williams who chaired the finance committee, "but there is a limit to how often our people should be asked to give. I think six special appeals a year is near that limit."

"If we raise more money for missions, that means less money for something else," reflected Jimmie Hall. "If we raise an extra $2,500 for world hunger, that means we're going to end up the year short in some other area. I'm afraid I will have to support the policy we adopted that limits special appeals to six a year. There's only so much money out there. We have to draw the line somewhere, and I believe six special appeals a year represents that line."

"My problem is a special appeal in early March will conflict with the special offering we always receive at Easter," objected Clara Phillips. "I'm afraid two special appeals that close together will compete with each other and neither will reach its goal."

"While I agree world hunger is a worthy cause and we should help alleviate it, I don't believe that's the issue before us tonight," declared Tim Griffin. "The real issue is stewardship. I'm convinced that if we could schedule an intensive stewardship education program here for the next two years, that would eliminate all of our financial problems. If we could teach our people to be good stewards of what God has given them, we could send fifty cents out of every dollar to missions."

"You've heard me say this before, but I feel compelled to bring it up again," commented Max Rizzo. "What we should do is go back to the system of a unified budget like we used to have here and eliminate all special offerings. Once you open the door to one or two special appeals, you'll always have people wanting to increase the number and ask for more. In the old days we used to go to our people once a year with everything in one budget and that was it. Every committee got a fair shake in the budget preparation process, and they had to live with what was allocated to that committee."

"That's not quite true, Max," objected Ruth Hawkins. "I've been a member here for nearly thirty years, and I can remember two different occasions when we followed the system of a unified budget we also had big special appeals. One was in 1972 for the building fund for the new educational wing, and a second came about ten years later to finish paying off that mortgage."

"Those were capital items and of course we had to have special appeals to raise that much money," patiently explained Max. "There's a big difference between special appeals for capital improvements and a unified budget for operating expenses."

"I have difficulty believing it is acceptable in the eyes of the Lord to have a special designated second-mile financial appeal for a new building for ourselves," challenged Ruth, "but unacceptable to the Lord to schedule a special appeal to help feed starving children."

After several seconds of embarrassed silence, the treasurer changed the subject by noting, "One thing that hasn't been mentioned is that as of August 31 we were still holding nearly $7,000 of bills we don't have the money to pay. I expect that by mid-October we

What are your assumptions?

—FRIAR TUCK

should be nearly caught up. The fact remains, however, that for the first three months of this fiscal year, which runs from the first of June through the end of May, our expenditures have exceeded our income by nearly $7,000. Maybe before we talk about helping others, we need to get our own financial house in order."

"Well, we only have two sources of income, contributions by our members to our regular budget and special appeals," summarized Pat Harrison. "The issue before us now is to act on this request for a seventh special offering for this fiscal year. Is anyone ready to offer a motion on this subject? We should get it settled tonight."

Pat Harrison was right. On the face of it that appeared to be the issue being raised by Hank Powell and the missions committee.

Pat Harrison was wrong. From a long-term policy-making perspective that was only a symptom of a far larger and more fundamental question that was being discussed. Instead of focusing their discussion on the request to approve an additional special offering, this group of policy-makers would have been well advised to review the basic assumptions on which they were basing their discussion. Several of those operational assumptions surfaced during this discussion. A review of ten of these operational assumptions will give you a chance to reflect on the assumptions on which the financial program in your congregation is based.

How Many Special Offerings?

The first of these assumptions to be raised came up when Pat Harrison referred to the rule limiting special appeals to six per year and when Terry Williams added there is a limit to how often people should be asked to give.

How are we going to direct our congregation's giving once they've seen TV?
—FRIAR TUCK

This assumes (a) it is good to place a limit on how often church members should be asked to contribute to charitable and religious causes and (b) the governing board of a congregation can and should protect the members against too many appeals.

This assumption includes at least two flaws. The most obvious is the governing board cannot limit the number of appeals to charitable causes made to the members of that congregation by televangelists, children's homes, colleges, the United Appeal, the Red Cross, radio preachers, and a variety of organizations that find direct mail appeals to be very productive. All the governing board at First Church can do is to declare, "We will limit the number of times we will ask our members for money and hope no one else will take advantage of that by asking our people to give to other causes." This approach assumes the governing board possesses far more authority than it really does.

A second, and far more serious flaw is that approach

**DIFFERENT HOPES
FOR
DIFFERENT FOLKS!**

*Is it really bad
to increase the choices
with which others
can be generous?*
—FRIAR TUCK

suggests the responsibility of the governing board is to limit the number of times the members can be asked to contribute and to limit the number and variety of causes members will be asked to support. A reasonably charitable description of this is that it is somewhere between counterproductive and dumb. A far more creative stance would be to trust the members to exercise good judgment, to challenge the people with a larger number and greater variety of needs and to let the members, not the governing board, choose among a larger number of congregationally sponsored appeals. The present system at First Church is designed to limit the amount of money members will contribute to and through First Church, to suggest the members' judgment cannot be trusted, and to increase the proportion of charitable giving by members that goes to causes totally unrelated to First Church. In general, the more limits the governing board places on what First Church will ask of its members, the larger the proportion of total member giving that will be directed to other charitable causes.

Is It a Fixed Sum Society?

A second, and perhaps the most profound issue that came up in this discussion, concerns the amount of money that people will contribute to charitable and religious causes. The limitation of six special offerings a year often is a product of the assumption that the financial resources can be represented by a pie, and if the number of slices is increased, each slice will be smaller in size. Jimmie Hall stated this most clearly, but it also was indirectly referred to by Terry Williams, Clara Phillips, Max Rizzo, and Pat Harrison.

"The four magic words that increase giving!"

—FRIAR TUCK.

Many church leaders assume that if additional money is allocated for one cause or need, some other committee or need will be shortchanged. The evidence suggests this is a completely fallacious assumption. Literally thousands of congregations have experienced a 30 to 100 percent increase in member giving within the space of twelve months without any significant change in the number of contributors.

The evidence indicates people respond to perceived needs, not to what they have been accustomed to giving. The response by the American people to the famine in Africa in 1985 is one recent example of this. Back after the end of World War II, when many congregations launched overdue building programs that had been postponed first by the Great Depression and next by the war, many denominational leaders feared these building programs would be funded at the expense of missions. It was widely assumed that since there was only so much money available, the increased expenditures for construction would result in decreased contributions for missions. Nearly all of the

... a courtship
where our needs
and the trust of others
can be rewarded!
—FRIAR TUCK

studies that were undertaken to test this assumption found that as expenditures for construction increased, total giving jumped to new levels and the money allocated for missions also rose. It is *not* a fixed-sum society!

Should People Have Choices?

An overlapping assumption that surfaced repeatedly in this discussion reflects a widely shared assumption that one responsibility of the governing board is to limit the number of choices available to the members. Some may argue this really is an issue of control, not simply of church finances. That may be true. Every year, for example, the governing boards of many churches decide to reduce the choices available to members on Sunday morning from two worship experiences to one service. In three cases out of four the result is a decrease in attendance, but everyone is reminded of who is in charge.

The decision to limit the number of special offerings to six a year and to require the missions committee to secure board approval for its proposed special appeal suggests that at First Church the operational assumption is that it is good to limit to a small number the choices available to people to contribute to needy causes.

By contrast, many congregations have discovered that an increase in the choices available to people is one means of increasing adult Sunday school attendance and/or increasing worship attendance and/or increasing financial contributions and/or increasing the number of participants in the women's organization and/or increasing the number of people who will volunteer to serve on committees or to teach in the Sunday school.

Is it good or bad to increase the choices available to people?

Is Stewardship the Basic Issue?

In the discussion at First Church Tim Griffin raised what many believe to be the basic issue when the issue of church finances is being discussed. This is the never-ending need for stewardship education.

Before examining that assumption, it is necessary to recognize one of the basic differences among Protestant congregations. A growing number can be described as high-expectation churches. These are the congregations that project high expectations of all members. These expectations often include strict adherence to certain doctrinal statements, a single position on baptism, agreement on criteria to be used in interpreting the Holy Scriptures, regular attendance at corporate worship, and a commitment to tithing, often with the stipulation that the tithe be returned to the Lord via the financial channels of that congregation. Contributions to other charitable causes must be above and beyond that tithe.

At the other end of that spectrum are the congregations that resemble voluntary associations. Members retain considerable autonomy in regard to their system of belief, their participation, the right of withdrawal, and their financial support. It is not at all uncommon for a substantial proportion of members to contribute less than five dollars a year, but retain all privileges of membership.

An effective stewardship education program in the high-expectation church may result in a substantial increase in member giving and most of that increase will be reflected in the total receipts of that congregation.

An even more effective stewardship education effort in a congregation at the voluntary association end of that spectrum may result in a doubling or tripling of the total contributions made to charitable and religious causes by the members, but only a modest amount of that increased giving may pass through the treasury of that congregation. In other churches an equally effective stewardship education program may produce a substantial increase in congregational receipts. The difference usually is in how clearly and forcefully the financial needs of that congregation are communicated to the members in comparison to other appeals made to the members for money. A good stewardship education program not only will motivate people to increase their level of giving, it also will teach them the responsibility of being good stewards of what God has given them and the need to be discriminating in where they direct their increased level of giving. Not all congregations earn the right to be perceived as good stewards of the contributor's gifts.

In today's world it is easy to find pastors, as well as

lay leaders, who contribute only a modest proportion of their total charitable contributions to the congregation of which they are members.

In at least one-third of all Protestant churches today the perceived financial crisis is not so much a product of a low level of giving by today's members as it is either (a) inadequate communication to the members of the financial needs of that congregation and/or (b) a low level of trust by a significant portion of the members in the policy-making processes or the financial system of that congregation.

For some churches the urgent need is an effective stewardship education program. For others it is an improvement in the quality of internal communication. For at least a few the most urgent need is to raise the level of trust between the members and the leaders.

Talking Ourselves into It

The most subtle issue raised by this discussion concerns procedure. The assumption communicated by Pat Harrison is that it is acceptable to have a proposal for change introduced and voted on at the same meeting. This assumes all present will have completed their best thinking on the subject by the time the vote is

taken. In the real world most normal people do their best thinking on the way home from the meeting.

Whenever people are asked to vote on a divisive or controversial issue at the same meeting at which it is first introduced, a common result is to reject it. The initial response to a new idea frequently is negative. The procedure being followed at First Church is biased, probably unintentionally, toward rejection of the proposal for a special offering for the relief of world hunger.

A common example of a better procedure is the series of educational efforts to inform all members of the cost of the proposed new building before anyone is asked to make a financial commitment to help pay for it. That series of letters, announcements, meetings, and visits is designed to give people time to talk themselves into becoming generous contributors to a cause they earlier might have supported with only a comparatively modest gift.

Back in the 1940s many young men used a procedure called "courtship" that was designed to give a particular young woman sufficient time to talk herself into saying yes before that young man proposed marriage. In recent years voters have been given an increasingly longer period of time to talk themselves into supporting a particular candidate's quest for the presidency of the United States.

What is the basic assumption you follow in your congregation? Do you believe people need time to talk themselves into supporting a proposal that will cost more money? Or are you satisfied with immediate responses?

Is the Unified Budget Obsolete?

During this discussion Max Rizzo raised an issue that traces back to the first quarter of the twentieth century. Is it best to have one budget that includes all causes and needs? Or is it best for each organization and group to have its own budget and raise its own funds? Or is it best to have one basic budget that covers most committees and organizations, but is supplemented with a small number of special appeals?

During the first three or four decades of the twentieth century it was a common practice in many denominations for representatives of various national boards and agencies of that denomination to make specific appeals to every congregation for financial support. Gradually this system was replaced with one appeal to each congregation with the understanding that the money given would be divided fairly among those several national denominational agencies and causes. The system of several appeals was replaced by a unified budget covering all participating agencies.

Concurrently a similar system was adopted in many cities as the United Appeal or United Fund replaced the dozens of individual financial appeals made by various charitable agencies to local merchants, corporations, and individuals.

During the 1930s and 1940s the concept of a unified budget was adopted by many congregations. In some

The unified budget
has such
a hollow sound
about it!

—FRIAR TUCK

churches a modified version of this was followed that consisted of (a) a three-pocket envelope with one pocket for contributions to the operating budget, a second pocket for contributions to the building fund, and a third pocket for missions, (b) weekly offerings in nearly every Sunday school class, and (c) completely separate and unrelated budgets and systems of financial support for the women's organization, the men's fellowship, and the youth group.

In fact, the unified budget rarely covered all facets of congregational giving and expenditures, but it became a popular concept.

The first big crack in the foundation of one unified budget to cover all expenditures was that big building program which often was financed by a major capital funds appeal conducted by a special committee rather than by the regular finance committee. When this worked, and it usually exceeded expectations, some people began to question the wisdom of the concept of a unified budget.

The second crack was the recognition that the unified budget often limited giving for missions. A common response was to authorize three to six special offerings every year with all proceeds designated for missions.

The third, and perhaps most devastating crack in the set of assumptions supporting this concept was inflation. When many congregations found their receipts were not increasing as rapidly as the increase in the consumer price index, the unified budget approach often required big cuts in certain areas. Typically the budget committee, after allocating funds for fixed costs such as utilities, insurance, salaries, Social Security, pensions, and health insurance, all of which rose rapidly year after year, found itself forced to cut the amount of money allocated to program, missions, advertising, evangelism, and the maintenance of the real estate. That, of course, turned out to be a loser and caused people to raise questions not only about the wisdom of a unified budget, but also about how to broaden the financial base. That leads us to question another assumption.

How Many Sources of Income Today?

In his closing comments back at First Church, Pat Harrison casually offered the broad generalization that only two sources of money were available, contributions by the members to the regular budget and special offerings. That generalization had some degree of validity in many congregations in 1955, but is an obsolete assumption in most churches today.

Thousands of Protestant congregations today report their annual receipts include several sources of money such as (1) contributions by members to the regular budget, (2) the loose offering, much of which may be contributed by visitors, (3) income from investments, (4) money received in special offerings for designated causes, (5) bequests, (6) user fees, (7) rentals for use of the real estate, (8) regular contributions from people who are not members, (9) receipts from money-raising activities, (10) loans, both short term and long term, (11) payments on pledges for next year or the following year, (12) grants from the denomination, (13) the sale of church-owned property, such as choir robes, stocks, bonds, land, air rights, church-owned houses, and goods donated to that church, (14) grants from individuals, local businesses, and foundations to help finance the cost of community programs such as child care, counseling centers, adult day care, shelters for the homeless and similar activities, and (15) grants and gifts from other churches.

If one looks back over the past twenty years the most rapidly growing segment of those channels of church income has been the increase in bequests. During the 1980s the fastest growing stream of income probably has been in user fees charged for the weekday nursery school, weddings, vacation Bible school, exercise classes, meals, Mother's Day Out, counseling services, off-street parking, child care, Bible study programs, field trips, music instruction, the Christian Day School, concerts, Sunday school, picnics, mission work camp trips, day camping experiences, and other activities.

While there is some overlap among these categories, to suggest that member contributions are the only source of local church income both oversimplifies a complex picture and offers an inadequate context for looking at ways to expand the financial base.

Surplus or Deficit?

The treasurer at First Church raised what may be the most interesting question in that entire discussion. Which is the better assumption? Is it good for a congregation to pay all bills on time and never run a deficit? That assumption usually requires building up at least a modest surplus to carry the church through those months when expenditures exceed receipts.

An alternative assumption is that it is somewhere

between necessary and desirable for a congregation to resolve one financial crisis only to be confronted by a new one and that cash flow squeeze is something that goes with the franchise like hot weather, annual vacations, the summer slump, and disputes over how loudly the organ should be played.

OH! OH!... WE'RE GOING DOWN *for* THE THIRD TIME *for* THE FIFTH TIME!

INCOME-OUT-GO

RED INK

Note: Healthy churches can have two to five financial crises a year!
—FRIAR TUCK

Adherents of the first assumption contend that a respectable church, like every other respectable business in town, pays its bills on time, maintains a surplus to cover emergencies, keeps expenditures within the limits of anticipated receipts, believes a smaller budget is a better budget than a bigger budget, and minimizes the cost of overhead.

Proponents of the second assumption point to scores of large, vigorous, vital, dynamic, enthusiastic, numerically growing, and apparently healthy congregations that often share a dozen characteristics. They (1) display a strong future orientation, (2) attract venturesome and risk-taking lay leaders, many of whom are first-generation Christians, (3) believe that if the Lord commands, the Lord will provide, (4) report an above average, for that denomination, ratio of worship attendance-to-membership, (5) respond readily and often eagerly to new challenges in ministry, even when the money does not appear to be readily available to finance those new ventures, (6) allocate an above

By the time we get
our house in order
it may be too late
to invite others in!

— FRIAR TUCK

average proportion of total receipts to missions, outreach, and community ministries, (7) enjoy bragging to others about the entrepreneurial gifts of their pastor, (8) offer a broad and varied program, (9) borrow money when wise counsel suggests that may not be appropriate at this time, (10) enjoy high visibility in the general community, (11) make many people in other congregations jealous of their vitality and appeal, and (12) encounter two to five financial crises every year, year after year. For some reason that is difficult to explain, rational, logical, and thoughtful observers who have difficulty comprehending why item (12) appears to be an essential component of that entire scenario.

By contrast it is easier to find numerically declining congregations that display these characteristics. They (1) reflect a strong past orientation, (2) report most of their policy-makers either were born into or married into that congregation, (3) offer people two choices—take it or leave it—, (4) find it easier to withhold permission than to grant approval, (5) display only limited enthusiasm for new ministries or new programs, (6) encounter difficulty in attracting and assimilating new members, especially persons born after 1945, (7) enjoy identifying and criticizing the inadequacies of their minister, (8) look back fondly to the days when the Sunday school was three times the size it is today and worship attendance was far above the current average, (9) attract cautious and fiscally conservative leadership, (10) report that between one-fifth and one-half of last year's total receipts came from (a) bequests and/or (b) income from investments and/or (c) the sale of real estate, and (11) end up the year with a comfortable surplus in the treasury.

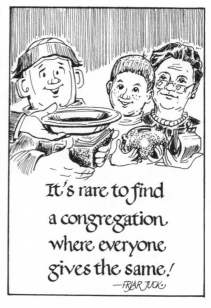

It's rare to find a congregation where everyone gives the same!
—FRIAR TUCK

These two long paragraphs can be dismissed as a pair of coincidences or they might influence your assumptions about deficits and surpluses.

Will Everyone Give the Same?

"Let's see now, we have seventy-three family units here in our church and our proposed budget for the next year comes to $58,980," calculated Paul Murphy. "If every family would contribute $832, that would cover everything."

"That's the dumbest thing I've ever heard!" declared Laurie Tompkins. "You know and I know that one-third of our members contribute at least two-thirds of the money we receive every year."

"That's true," admitted Paul, "But that's not how it should be. I believe the load should be divided up evenly among all our people."

What do you believe? What is your basic assumption as you plan for next year? That everyone should and will contribute about the same? Or do you accept as a fact that in the typical healthy congregation one-third of the members will contribute approximately two-thirds of all contributions received?

Your basic assumption on this question will influence your plans and your expectations.

What Are the Sources of Members' Contributions?

"We've checked both the *Sales Management* estimates and the census reports, and we are convinced the median family income of the members of this congregation is at least $30,000 annually," explained the stewardship consultant to Calvary Church. "Last year your 143 family units contributed a combined total of $114,743 or an average of slightly over $800 per family. If the median family income is at least $30,000 a year, that means you probably have many families with above $50,000 a year bracket, especially with as many two-income families as you have here at Calvary Church. Therefore we estimate the total income of your families was at least $6.7 million last year. That means the stewardship level of the people was only 1.7 percent. That's a long way from the biblical tithe, and we believe there is an urgent need for a strong stewardship education program in this congregation. You should be able to expect your people to give at least at the national level of 2.2 percent of their income, and 1.7 percent is far below that!"

From the listener's perspective there are three things wrong with that brief speech. First, it is likely to antagonize a number of the members who are generous contributors. Second, it assumes that all charitable contributions made by the members go to Calvary

Church. As was pointed out earlier, that often is not true. The higher the income level, the more likely that person or household will distribute their charitable giving to a variety of causes. Only in (a) lower income households and (b) some high expectation churches are most of the charitable contributions of the members channeled to and through the church treasury. It is not uncommon for higher income members of voluntary association type churches to allocate well over one-half of their total charitable contributions to causes and organizations other than to the church to which they belong. This pattern of giving is encouraged by many denominational officials who make direct appeals to loyal members with high incomes to make contributions that never appear in their congregation's financial records.

Perhaps the most misleading assumption in that brief speech, however, is the clear implication that people contribute to charitable causes out of their current income. That was true for the overwhelming majority of Americans in 1950 and probably is true for a majority today. A rapidly growing number of Americans of all ages, however, today have accumulated substantial wealth, usually referred to as "savings" or "investments" or "our house" or "our farm" or "our business."

It is not at all unusual for over one-half of the money received in a congregation's special building fund campaign to come out of the savings of accumulated wealth of their members. An increasing number of churches report that a growing proportion of the contributions to the annual operating expenses come in the form of stock certificates and other forms of accumulated wealth; to assume that members can and will contribute to the church only out of their current income is to place a serious limitation on expectations!

What are the assumptions on which the financial program of your congregation is built? Do some of these assumptions need to be articulated in precise terms so they can be evaluated? Do some need to be challenged? That may be the next decision for your leaders before you begin to choose from among forty-four ways to expand the financial base of your congregation.

CHAPTER TWO

Teaching Stewardship

When Larry was three, we gave him an allowance every week," recalled Stacy Davis, the forty-six-year-old mother of three sons. "My husband, Jack, and I wanted to teach our children four concepts. One was responsibility; sooner or later every one of us must accept the responsibility for our earlier actions. Sometimes that's called growing up. A second was stewardship. A third was deferred gratification. The fourth was competence in financial matters."

"That's placing a heavy load on the simple matter of a weekly allowance, isn't it?" asked Stacy's neighbor. "Tell me more."

"Every week we gave Larry a quarter, two dimes, and a nickel," explained Stacy. "We told him the quarter had to go into his savings jar. As soon as that jar contained twenty quarters, we told him that he could buy anything he wanted. The two dimes he could blow in immediately on anything his little heart desired. It only took two rounds of filling up that jar with twenty quarters before Larry learned about the benefits of savings and the concept of deferred gratification. It doesn't take a three-year-old long to learn that five dollars will purchase more than twenty cents will buy.

"The nickel," continued Stacy, "represented his tithe from his allowance and went into the church jar. When he began getting a weekly allowance, we asked our church for a box of envelopes that would be for Larry's tithe. When a couple of the members of the finance committee discovered his tithe was only five cents, they

—FRIAR TUCK·

Blessed are they who teach
their children to tithe
for they shall produce adults
who can lovingly
assign their assets!

objected. One objected that the cost of a box of envelopes was too much to waste on someone who only gave $2.60 a year. The other objected because of the extra work for the counters every Sunday to open an envelope, take out a nickel, and record it. Their objections, however, were offset by the enthusiasm Larry displayed every week as he impatiently waited for the ushers to pass the offering plate."

"Larry may be the only person I've ever known, except for a few preachers," observed the neighbor, "who was eager to have the offering taken up in church!"

"The point is that now Larry is twenty-one years old, and Jack and I are convinced he learned all of those four abstract concepts by the way he handled his allowance. We have followed the same system with both of our other boys and we believe it works."

How Do You Teach?

While some readers may question whether fifty cents a week was the appropriate allowance for a three-year-old boy twenty years ago, that is not the point of the story. The central point is there are many different ways of teaching stewardship. Some may add that parents are the most influential teacher the young child ever has. Others may point out that concepts taught in the preschool years are more likely to be internalized than those taught in adulthood. The cynics and those without a strong future orientation may object that teaching three-year-olds to drop a nickel in the offering plate every week will not solve today's financial problems. It may, however, be the most

Leaders who tithe....

Our models in living
can be
our motivators in giving!

—FRIAR TUCK

effective means of teaching stewardship to the church leaders of the year 2019.

Leaders Tithe and Tithers Lead

What may be the second most effective approach to teaching stewardship to people in your church also may arouse considerable opposition. As a growing number of Protestant congregations have decided to become tithing churches, some have adopted the slogan "Leaders Tithe and Tithers Lead."

Three versions of this concept are reasonably common. The strictest limits the list of volunteers who will be asked to serve on administrative or program committees or teaching in the Sunday school to members who are known to be tithers. In some congregations the signing of a card declaring, "I am a tither," followed by an explanation of that concept is

sufficient. In at least a few churches all proposed nominees are cleared with the financial secretary to be sure they are tithers.

A less restrictive expression of this concept is implemented by a number of Presbyterian churches that require all members of the Session, but not all committee members or Sunday school teachers, to be tithers. In simple terms, the only members eligible for election as elders in these churches are tithers.

The most common version is to phase the policy in over two or three or four years. The new policy applies only to persons to be elected, or reelected, to a new term of office. They are drawn only from among those who tithe. Persons completing a term of office are not required to tithe in order to complete that term in office, but they must be tithers to be eligible for reelection.

This approach to teaching stewardship assumes (a) modeling is the most powerful teaching tool available for use in the church and (b) leaders should model what is considered in that congregation to be acceptable behavior.

Is the Minister a Model?

Overlapping this is a very widely used and highly effective approach to teaching stewardship. This is based on three critical assumptions, (1) the minister is the most influential teacher among the adults in that congregation and by word and deed models acceptable behavior patterns for all members, (2) the minister is committed to the idea of tithing and is a tither, and (3) the minister is both able and willing to urge members to adopt tithing as a way of life.

Some will argue this is not only the most effective means of teaching tithing, but also is an essential block in the foundation of any systematic approach to stewardship education in the local church.

New Beginnings Teach New Habits

Several pastors have discovered their most effective approach to stewardship education is in the extended class for adult new members. Typically this class is composed of adults who are prospective new members and meets weekly for twenty-four or thirty-two or forty-five weeks. In those congregations receiving a large number of new members every year one class may meet on Sunday morning, the next class, which begins several weeks later, meets on Tuesday evenings, a third class may meet on Saturday mornings, and a fourth class may gather on Thursday evenings. This offers prospective new members a choice of meeting times.

Typically the curriculum consists of several components. One may be on what Christians believe, another on the Bible, a third on church history, a fourth on the origins and teachings of that denominational family, a fifth on the history and culture of that congregation, a sixth on stewardship, a seventh on the program of that congregation, an eighth on missions, and a ninth on a subject dear to that pastor's heart. Each unit requires two to six weeks.

In some churches a team of three lay volunteers leads

one class through that entire sequence. A second team of three lay volunteers leads another class and so on. The congregation may include three or four experts on certain subjects. This local expert teaches the unit on the Bible to every class. This local expert teaches the unit on the history of that particular congregation to every class and another local expert teaches the unit on stewardship. The pastor may or may not be heavily involved with every class.

Among the benefits several stand out repeatedly. This is an exceptionally effective means of assimilating new members. This extended class enables new members to meet and make new friends. This system can produce a group of exceptionally knowledgeable lay leaders as a result of each three-person team leading two or three classes through this process. This approach often means the average giving of all recent new members exceeds the average level of giving by all other members. (In the typical Protestant congregation today new members do not reach the congregation-wide level of giving until their third or fourth year of membership—this process can accelerate that pace.) The primary purposes of the extended new members' class usually are (a) assimilating and (b) enabling new members to become knowledgeable members. Both goals usually are achieved. Finally, this can be a useful

component of the preaching schedule over the next two or three years. Persuasive preaching can be a powerful force in changing both beliefs and behavior!

Stewardship Preaching

"This is the beginning of a fifty-two part sermon series on stewardship and giving!"

—FRIAR TUCK

Proportional Giving

Another widely used stewardship concept is to encourage members to think in terms of proportional giving as a preliminary step to an increase in the number of tithers. It is not at all uncommon to find many active and heavily involved church members who contribute only 2 or 3 percent of their income to the congregation to which they belong. This approach urges those now contributing 2 percent of their income to raise that to 3 percent next year, those now contributing 3 percent are encouraged to increase it to 4 percent. Everyone is asked to increase the proportion of income he or she contributes to that church by one percentage point each year. Thus in five years the person now contributing 2 percent will be contributing 7 percent.

Two cautions must be raised about this stewardship approach. The first is: do not set unrealistic goals. Sometimes this is publicized as a means of creating a tithing church in less than a decade. That might happen if this is a congregation that does not lose any members or gain any new ones during that decade. Most congregations will lose at least 20 percent of the current membership during the next decade and many will lose 30

STEP UP to STEWARDSHIP!

Tithers aren't born...
instead they grow
a percentage point a year!

—FRIAR TUCK

to 60 percent. That turn-over means this can be a goal, but not a destination unless every potential new member is required to become a tither before being admitted to full membership. (That is a requirement for member-ship in at least 5,000 churches in North America.)

The second and more serious caution applies when the outside stewardship consultant comes in, checks the data from *Sales Management* or the Bureau of the Census to ascertain the average household income in this community, computes the per member giving *to that church* of the members and declares, "The level of stewardship here is a disgrace! The giving level here is only 2 percent of the income level of the members." That broad generalization may offend the tithers among the membership. It is even more likely to offend the self-identified faithful stewards who contribute 8 to 15 percent of their income to charitable causes, but only a small fraction of their total giving is routed through the records of that parish. The closer the congregation is to the voluntary association end on that spectrum of churches that has the high-expectation congregations at one end and those churches that resemble voluntary associations at the other end, the more likely that only a relatively small fraction of the members' combined total giving to charitable causes goes into the offering plates of that congregation.

Improve Internal Communication

For a great many congregations, especially those toward the voluntary association end of that spectrum, an effective stewardship approach will focus on improving the quality of internal communication between that congrega-

Tithing...

...god's way of using just enough of our money to cause us to pray over how we spend all the rest!

—FRIAR TUCK.

tion as an institution and the individual members. One facet of that internal communication system can be stewardship education. A second can be to improve the quality of two-way communication so the members believe they are being heard. The three-call system described in chapter 6 can be an effective means of helping all members believe they are being heard. A third facet of this approach is persuasive communication to the members about the financial needs of that congregation. The fourth, and sometimes the most crucial facet of this approach, involves the words "authentic" and "trust." The information received by people must be credible, trustworthy, authentic, believable, and accurate. If the information conveyed to members is perceived by the recipients of those messages as exaggerated, unreliable, or inaccurate, the foundation for a good stewardship program can be quickly and thoroughly eroded.

Stewardship education should be an integral part of any effort to strengthen the financial base of your congregation, but some congregations also need to take immediate action to raise the level of member giving. The most dramatic means of accomplishing that is the big special appeal.

CHAPTER THREE

Three Major Special Appeals

"I don't believe many of our people question the need for more space," observed Ray Willis, "but I do know a lot of people who have serious doubts about our ability to finance a $160,000 building program."

"Well, there's only one way to find out," declared Grace Evans, the vigorous, sixty-eight-year-old widow of a lifelong member of this 387-member congregation located in a midwestern county seat town of 2,900 residents. Grace had been born and reared in Rhode Island and had moved to this community when she was twenty-four to work as the office nurse for a physician. Several years later she had married a widower, the son of the man who owned the local hardware store. For her first four years in town she had been knows as "Doc Roger's nurse." Subsequently, she often was referred to as "young Ben Evans' second wife." Eventually, however, the stigma of being an outsider wore off and Grace had earned her place as a respected member of the community and as an influential leader in this ninety-eight-year-old congregation. Therefore no one questioned it when she was asked to serve as one of the seven members of the recently appointed Building Facilities Committee to study the real estate needs of this congregation. After several months the committee members had concluded they would recommend a modest remodeling of the structure completed in 1924 and the addition of a two-story wood frame structure that would provide a suite of offices and one large meeting room on the first floor with three classrooms

Stewardship Decisions

YES

Only the "yeses" can bless us!
—FRIAR TUCK

on the second floor. A contractor on the committee estimated the total cost at $150,000 to $160,000. (When it was completed, the actual total expenditures came to $213,800 including furnishings, but everyone was so pleased with the additional facilities that very few complaints were heard about the actual costs exceeding the estimate.)

"What's your suggestion, Grace, for finding out?'' asked another member of the committee.

"I think we ought to hold a referendum,'' replied Grace. "I've been told you should have at least one-half of the money in hand when you go into a building program. So let's go to the members and tell them we have before us a motion to build an addition, that we estimate the cost to be $160,000, the motion has been seconded, 80,000 votes are required to approve that motion, the votes are a dollar apiece, you can vote as many times as you want, the polls will be open for one year, if we get 80,000 votes, we go ahead; if we don't have the $80,000 at the end of one year, we return the money to the donors and forget the whole deal.''

"Where in the world did you ever get an idea like that?'' challenged another member of the committee.

"A cousin of mine back East wrote me last month that they had done this and it had worked for them,'' explained Grace. "She wrote that instead of having a congregational meeting, where there would be a lot of choosing up of sides and the negative votes wouldn't get anything done, they had decided to count only the yes votes. She's a member of a congregation a little smaller than ours and they raised over $60,000 in four months toward a $90,000 renovation program. They borrowed the other $30,000 and went ahead with the project without ever asking the people who opposed it to vote against it."

"We couldn't do that here," cautioned a lifelong member. "Our constitution requires us to have a congregational vote on anything like what we're talking about here. We would have to give the opponents a chance to voice their opposition."

"I'm well aware of that," replied Grace, "but we don't need to hold that congregational meeting until we have a specific building proposal to present to the members. We can go ahead and ask for the yes votes and count them without a congregational meeting. If we raise enough money in advance, the congregational meeting should be only a formality to approve what our people already have decided they will support."

Eleven weeks and four meetings later the Building Facilities Committee took Grace's proposal to the members. Twelve months later a total of 117,845 yes votes, at one dollar each, had been received, counted, and banked. During that year, the Committee went ahead and had detailed plans prepared for the proposed addition. The low bid came in at $188,300. When this specific proposal was presented to the required congregational meeting, the motion to accept that bid and proceed with construction carried 119 to 4 in secret balloting.

*   *   *

"Our big problem in preparing a budget for next year is that we begin with a given of $58,000 for mortgage payments," complained Herb Jensen, a member of the Finance Committee at the 503-member First Church. "We're projecting receipts of $228,000 for this coming year, and a fourth of that goes for debt service. If we didn't have these mortgage payments, we could add the second staff person we need so

badly, increase our mission giving, and give both our secretary and the custodian a healthy salary increase."

"Well, in another five years we'll have the mortgage paid off and we can do some catching up," observed Rachel Hernandez.

"I have a better idea," piped up thirty-seven-year-old Pat Hagan, who had joined First Church less than two years earlier and did not know newcomers should not offer radical proposals. "The amount we still owe on that mortgage is approximately $175,000. Why don't we have a special campaign to raise $175,000, pay off the mortgage, and that will free up $58,000 for other needs as we prepare the budget?"

After a ten-minute discussion, Pat's suggestion was dismissed as completely unrealistic, and the committee went back to the task of trying to make an anticipated $228,000 in receipts cover needs that exceeded $270,000.

Two weeks later, at the next meeting of the finance committee Pat once again brought up the possibility of a special financial campaign to raise $175,000 and pay off the mortgage. Rachel was the only one to support Pat's suggestion.

Two weeks later Pat brought up the idea at another meeting of that committee and was pleased to see two more supporters speak in favor of it, but nothing happened. The preparation of the budget dominated the agenda.

Six months later, and two months after the beginning of the new fiscal year, the leaders at First Church decided to schedule a Miracle Sunday for the second weekend in May. The goal was to raise $155,000 to pay off what would still remain from that $500,000 mortgage taken out several years earlier to finance the expansion of the physical facilities.

The strategy included creation of a thirty-five-member general committee with a seven-person steering committee. The other twenty-eight members were persons who, it was hoped, would be major contributors to this appeal. A series of six letters were mailed to all members. All were mailed with the expectation they would arrive on a Tuesday, when residential first class mail tends to be minimal.

Each letter was signed in brightly colored ink by the

It's different letters
from different
people that make
a real difference!
—FRIAR TUCK

person who wrote it. Each of the first five letter writers added a personal postscript in colored ink to the bottom of each letter. That added a personal touch to what in fact was a form letter.

Each envelope carried in the upper lefthand corner the name and address of the sender, not the church's name and address. People are more interested in mail that comes from individuals than mail sent by institutions. Each letter was mailed first class and carried a colorful commemorative stamp in the upper right hand corner. Every envelope was addressed by the word processor in the church office. No labels were used.

Each letter was individually typed on that word processor with the name and address of the recipient at the top. At the very top of the 6" x 9" personal size stationery the word processor printed in the name and address of the sender of that round of letters. Each letter was limited to approximately 125 words per page and ran three or four pages in length.

The first letter was written by the individual who chaired this special committee and who was a widely respected and influential member of First Church. The theme of that first letter was, "Friends, we are in a severe financial squeeze here at First Church, and the best solution to the problem is to eliminate those big monthly mortgage payments from our budget. The way to do that is a special appeal to pay off the mortgage."

The second letter came from a seventy-two-year-old widely respected and influential third-generation member of First Church. It repeated, in different words, the theme of the first letter and added the point about how much money could be saved in interest costs by paying off the mortgage in advance. The first five letters were mailed at two-week intervals.

The third letter came from the overworked pastor who blessed the whole plan with an inspirational stewardship message.

The fourth letter discussed the question, How much is $155,000? and pointed out the answer was NOT a check for $600 for each of the 260 households at First Church. The writer of this fourth letter explained that to reach the goal of $155,000 the committee had concluded three gifts of at least $10,000 each would be needed as well as five contributions of at least $5,000 each, at least fifteen of $2,500 each, and twenty-five of $1,000 each in addition to the scores of contributions that would range from $5 to $500.

The committee recognized that 80 percent of the dollars in this type of appeal usually comes from 20 percent of the householders and this letter offered the array of choices to make that happen. To be more specific, the letter projected that 48 contributors (19 percent of the member households) would give a combined total of approximately $120,000 (77 percent of the goal). When the results were added up, it turned out that the top fifty-two contributors gave a combined total of $128,000 or 80.5 percent of the $159,000 actually received.

Incidentally, this letter did offend two or three members who were convinced that $5 to $10 contributions were not wanted and would not count for much in the eyes of the committee, but would be perceived as of equal value in God's eyes.

The fifth letter carried a "get on the band wagon" message and came from a layperson on the committee. It opened with the words, "As you all know, we expect to raise $155,000 in cash on Mother's Day. Some of you have told me this is an impossible goal. Others have said we will be lucky if we receive $50,000 that day. A couple of my pessimistic friends have declared this whole program is a dumb idea and the most we can expect is $25,000 or $30,000 in a one-day appeal like this. Well, friends, we have news for you! Miracle Sunday is still nearly two weeks away and already we have nearly $63,000 in hand in advance commitments! One family has promised us a check for $15,000 if the rest of us contribute the other $140,000 we need to pay off that dirty old mortgage."

The next two pages of that letter were a plea for people to rally behind the goal that was already in sight.

The reason this letter was possible was because members of that thirty-five-member steering committee had been asked to make advance commitments. Those who responded early gave that combined total of nearly $63,000. One member stated his family would hand over a check for $15,000 if the rest of the congregation gave a combined total of $140,000 by noon on the Monday following Mother's Day. That added an extra incentive.

The sixth letter was prepared late Sunday afternoon on Mother's Day and was mailed on Monday morning. Every copy was personally signed, in various colors of ink, by the pastor, the person who had chaired the committee, and the members who had written the second and fifth letters.

This letter announced the results, thanked the

people, and devoted the last two pages to an explanation of how the success of this effort would enable First Church to expand its ministry and outreach. The pastor insisted the central focus should not be on $155,000, but rather on gratitude to God, on the loyalty and support of the members, and on an expansion of ministry.

FOR THE FOURTH YEAR IN A ROW, I RISE TO...

The idea of relocation may be rejected many times before it is accomplished!

—FRIAR TUCK

*   *   *

During a twenty-seven-year period Trinity Church had seen eight different ministers come and go. This 281-member congregation had been formally organized in 1899 and the present Akron-plan sanctuary had been constructed in 1905. A six-room Sunday school wing was added in 1923. The congregation peaked in size in 1926 with an average attendance of 217 in Sunday school and 185 in worship. After a quarter century of gradual decline a new, young, energetic, creative, and charming minister arrived in 1951. Four years later the congregation was averaging 175 at worship and 165 in Sunday school. Following his departure in 1962, the congregation experienced a succession of what were widely perceived as mismatches between young ministers and an aging membership.

In 1971 the fourth minister in this series proposed that Trinity Church sell its property, which covered slightly less than two-thirds of an acre, and relocate to a

IT ONLY HURTS WHEN I STOP!

BRICK WALL

Persistent and patient pastors produce positive possibilities!
—FRIAR TUCK

new and larger site west of town and construct a new meeting place.

The response to this sign of discontent was a decision to give the minister a housing allowance and remodel the parsonage next door to the church into a parish hall with separate offices for the minister and secretary. Worship attendance continued to decline and Sunday school attendance dropped even faster.

A few years later the next pastor asked for the creation of a special long-range planning committee. After fourteen months of study this committee recommended relocation. Nothing happened.

Several years later another new minister encouraged creation of a special committee to study the future of Trinity Church. After nearly two years of discussion, the decision was made to invest $22,000 in renovating the sanctuary including new carpeting and matching pew cushions.

About three years ago a new minister arrived, analyzed the situation, enlisted allies from among those who earlier had recommended relocation, and created an ad hoc study committee that recommended relocation. That entire process took nearly three years. Within the next fifteen months the people at Trinity Church had (a) voted by a 4-1 margin to relocate, (b) purchased a five-acre relocation site six miles to the west for

$73,000, (c) paid for that site with a small scale, low key financial campaign that raised $48,000 and with $25,000 "borrowed" from the endowment fund, and (d) secured the services of a professional fund-raiser who came in and directed a three-year campaign that raised $86,000 in cash plus $189,000 in pledges against the $250,000 total goal. The pledges were to be paid over three years.

A year later the construction of the first unit of a $600,000 building was under way. The old property was sold to a six-year-old Pentecostal congregation that had been renting space in a commercial building and was seeking a permanent church. The trustees at Trinity Church had hired an appraiser who placed a fair market value of $30,000 on the land and appraised the church building and the parish house at $195,000 on the basis of reproduction value minus depreciation. When she presented her report, the appraiser warned the trustees, "Don't automatically reject any offer because it is way below the appraisal. In this part of the city the market demand for obsolete buildings is very limited, and the supply exceeds the demand. If I were in your shoes and someone offered me $90,000, I would take it. Remember, when it comes to old church buildings, there can be a big difference between fair market value and reproduction costs minus depreciation."

The Pentecostal congregation offered $85,000, the trustees insisted the rock bottom price was $125,000, and the two parties compromised on a sale price of $100,000 that allowed Trinity Church to take five stained-glass windows, replace them with new clear windows and also to take all the chancel furniture.

This story of Trinity Church illustrates a half-dozen generalizations. The most obvious is that proposals for relocation of the meetingplace often are rejected repeatedly before relocation actually takes place. A second generalization is that most aging congregations prefer the status quo to change. A third is that radical change, such as relocation, usually requires the patient and persistent initiative of a pastor who is willing and able to lead. A fourth is that congregations usually underestimate their resources and potential. A fifth is that old church buildings rarely sell for what it costs to replace them, even after allowing for depreciation. A sixth is that when a group of committed church members do make a decision and decide to implement that new course of action, the pace of change can be far more rapid than most people would have believed possible five years earlier.

This chapter, however, is not about the relocation of a congregation's meeting place. The theme of this chapter is about major special financial appeals.

The three examples described here, each one of which is drawn from real life, illustrate several basic generalizations about this approach to expanding a congregation's financial base.

The first, and by far the most important, is that there is only one effective way for a congregation to raise a large amount of money in a brief period of time. That is to ask for it. Everything else is an elaboration of that fundamental point. Most people will not contribute large sums of money to any cause or organization unless they are asked to do so.

In this first example Grace Evans suggested the use of the "count the yes votes" method and a large amount of money was raised in one year. At First Church the decision was to use the Miracle Sunday appeal. Literally dozens of Protestant congregations raised at least one million dollars in one day during the 1980s with a Miracle Sunday appeal.

At Trinity Church the leaders chose to utilize the traditional three-year building fund campaign approach with the guidance of a professional fund-raiser. This was more widely utilized in the 1950–80 period than today, but it remains a useful alternative.

The common theme of all three methods was to ask the members to make large contributions.

The second basic generalization is that the vast majority of church members make their weekly or monthly financial contribution to their church out of current income. The major special financial appeal is one means of asking some members to contribute out of accumulated wealth. (See chapter 1 for an elaboration of this point.)

Some church members have regular income, but little accumulated wealth. Many have what their great

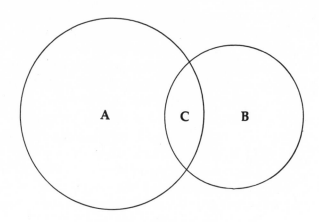

grandparents would describe as an amazingly high level of current income and an unbelievably large amount of accumulated wealth. Others have a modest level of current income but considerable accumulated wealth. A common result of this three-part division of the membership is that some people are able to give generously out of their current income, but not able to make a large contribution to a major special appeal. They are represented by the large circle A in the box to the left. Others contribute rather modestly out of their weekly income to the regular budget, but are able and willing, when challenged, to make a large contribution out of their savings to a special appeal. They are represented by the smaller circle B in the box. A few are able and willing both to be generous contributors out of their current income to the regular budget and also occasionally to make large gifts out of their accumulated wealth. They are represented by the overlap or C of these two circles.

Obviously, the relative size of these two circles and the proportion of members who fit into the overlapping section may vary greatly from one congregation to another.

This major special financial appeal can be an effective means of expanding your congregation's financial base by asking for contributions from accumulated wealth.

A third and overlapping generalization is based on the fact that in the healthy congregation approximately one-third of the members contribute two-thirds of the money given by members. (This will not be the same as two-thirds of total receipts in those congregations where a large proportion of total income is derived from rents, income from investments, user fees, and other sources.)

In many congregations one-fourth of the members account for three-fourths of the contributions from members. Frequently, that is a source of concern about an excessively narrow financial base. When one-fifth of the members contribute four-fifths of the total operating budget, that may be a cause of alarm. That extreme pattern in contributions to the regular operating budget usually is a symptom of a more serious internal problem.

> OFFERTORY MUSIC HAS AN INCREDIBLE, SHRINKING EFFECT ON MANY *of* US!

Note: One-third *of* the members *of* a healthy congregation give as much money as all the rest!

—*FRIAR TUCK*

By contrast, when the sources of contributions for a major special financial appeal are identified, it is not at all uncommon to discover that 20 percent of the contributors accounted for 80 percent of the money received. This is a more common pattern in the brief appeal, such as Miracle Sunday, than in the traditional three-year capital funds campaign. The reason for that 80-20 division, of course, is that the success of the brief appeal usually is related to people giving out of accumulated wealth rather than out of current income.

That means that your leaders probably should be alarmed if 80 percent of the contributions to your regular operating budget come from only 20 percent of your members. If, however, 80 percent of the money received in a Miracle Sunday appeal comes from only 20 percent of the members, you usually are free to describe that as a normal and predictable pattern.

A big factor behind the declining attractiveness of the traditional three-year building fund campaign is that it

Ask for the moon and get it!

was based on the assumption that few members had accumulated much wealth and most could contribute only out of current income.

The rapid increase in recent years in the number of church members who possess substantial accumulated wealth is the chief reason for the growing appeal of the Miracle Sunday approach.

A fourth generalization about major special appeals that was illustrated by these three case studies is that the leadership of the vast majority of congregations in American Protestantism tends to place unrealistically low ceilings on their expectations. This broad generalization has many facets and includes expectations about major special financial appeals. Repeatedly the amount contributed exceeds the stated goal by a substantial amount. All too often low expec-

tations produce results that could have been exceeded by more optimistic goals.

The fifth generalization is that the amount that can be raised in a major special financial appeal varies greatly. It may range from an amount equal to one-half of total member giving for the previous year to three times that amount.

GULP!
SPECIAL APPEALS HELP — NOT HURT!

LOVE PLEASE

"Giving does beget giving!"
—FRIAR TUCK

The three-year capital funds drive often produced an amount equal to two-and-one-half times the regular budget. The usual range for Miracle Sunday is very broad—from one-third of last year's member giving to over three times that amount. Counting the yes votes rarely produces an amount in excess of one year's regular budget.

A sixth generalization is that adequate time should be allowed to plan the special appeal, for the use of redundant communication to the members about the need and the goal, and to allow people to talk themselves into supporting it.

If a widespread perception of a serious crisis exists, this can be a matter of weeks. If a high degree of satisfaction with the status quo and complacency dominate the climate, several years may be required to increase the level of discontent and to mobilize a support group.

Seventh, it cannot be emphasized too strongly that

Many a church...

MIRACLE SUNDAY!

is no longer adrift because of the lift of one great gift!

— FRIAR TUCK

the goal influences the response. This may be a broad congregation-wide goal, or it may be spelled out in more detail as was done through that fourth letter in the Miracle Sunday approach used at First Church.

As one veteran leader at First Church commented after the successful conclusion of their appeal, "If we had done this three years ago when the mortgage was about $260,000, we would have raised $260,000." Expectations and goals do influence performance!

Finally, a word of caution needs to be raised. If your congregation currently is torn by severe internal dissension, this may not be the appropriate time for a major financial appeal. Likewise, if the cause or need is perceived as highly divisive or controversial, this may not be the appropriate approach to raising the money for it.

CHAPTER FOUR

Eleven Minor Special Appeals

"The Wiley College choir will be singing here next Sunday evening and there's nothing in the budget for that. Has anyone done anything yet to make sure we can at least cover their travel costs?" anxiously asked one of the members of Wesley Lutheran Church.

"Oh, that's not a problem," came the instant reply. "We'll take up a special offering that evening and give them everything that is received."

The Appeal of That Sacred Place

"It's one thing to talk about a 99 percent vote of support at a congregational meeting for this proposal to buy the property next door to the church, raze the house, and pave the lot for additional off-street parking. It's another question of how we'll get the money to pay for all of that," challenged a long-time member of the 1800-member Bethany Church.

"Oh, that won't be any problem, that's peanuts," replied a member of the committee that had originated the proposal. "We'll need about $105,000 to cover all the costs. When you put that next to our $800,000 annual budget, that's really a modest amount of money. We'll mail a letter to every member household next month spelling out the need and enclosing an envelope for an extra offering. On the basis of our past experience here at Bethany I expect we'll have the whole $105,000 within two or three weeks. That's not really a big deal for a congregation of our size." A month after that letter had been mailed, the treasurer had received checks and cash from nearly four hundred households that totaled $108,435. For the vast majority of Protestant congregations that would have been a major appeal, but at Bethany Church it was perceived as a minor appeal.

These two conversations illustrate two of the most common and widely used means of using a special offering to expand a congregation's financial base. One is to receive a special offering to remunerate a visiting choir or evangelist or speaker or to cover some expense not included in the budget. A second is the special offering to improve the quality of our sacred meeting-place. In both cases a persuasive argument can be offered for keeping that need out of the budget and handling it by a special appeal. Under this broad umbrella it is easy to identify several additional types of minor special appeals.

The Regular Annual Appeal

A third and perhaps the least controversial and most common of these minor special financial appeals are those regular annual special offerings for a specific cause. In tens of thousands of congregations these annual special offerings have become institutionalized and are an unchallenged component of that church's religious subculture.

In terms of size and the amount of money given the two big examples of this are both found in the Southern Baptist Convention. The annual Lottie Moon appeal raised more than $69 million for world missions in 1986 and the Annie Armstrong offering produced nearly $28 million for home missions in that same year.

On a more modest scale many churches have

institutionalized the tradition of a special offering on Christmas Eve,
Easter Sunday, World
Communion Sunday,
Thanksgiving, and per-
haps three or four other
occasions every year.
More often than not, the
proceeds from these reg-
ular special appeals are
earmarked for some be-
nevolent or missional
cause and over a period
of time can result in a
substantial increase in
the amount of money
allocated to missions.

Once special, designated appeals are institutionalized, they become difficult to abandon!
—FRIAR TUCK

Like the sales tax, some people see these designated
special appeals as a nuisance. Others see them, like the
sales tax, as a relatively simple and painless way to raise
extra money. Like the sales tax, once they have been
institutionalized, it is extremely difficult to abandon
them.

Make Up the Deficit

"The treasurer has told us that for the first eleven
months of the year our expenditures have exceeded our
income by nearly $4,000," announced the minister one
Sunday evening. "We still have to pay the rest of our
commitments for missions so the Board has decided to
take up a special offering next Sunday morning to make
up the deficit and make sure all our obligations are paid
in full before the end of the year. You'll receive a letter
in the mail this week describing our needs in more

BY A VOTE OF THIRTEEN *to* TWELVE, THE BOARD HAS VOTED TO PAY ITS BENEVOLENCE OBLIGATIONS FOR YOUR RELEASE!

Ransom the Minister

detail and a special offering envelope will be enclosed. Please pray over this before you make a decision about how much you can give. This church has always ended the year with all bills paid, and we don't want this to be the first year we fail to do that."

This appeal, based on pride, prayer, need, and the congregation's reputation for always responding when a genuine need surfaced, brought in $4,721 the following Sunday. No one was surprised, but all were pleased.

Ransom the Minister

"I've been in the ministry for twenty-nine years, and everywhere I've ever served, that congregation has always paid its apportionments in full," declared the senior minister at Asbury United Methodist Church one Sunday morning, "and I'm not about to break that record. While the law of our church states the minister must be paid first, I've told our Board and the treasurer that I will not accept my salary check unless all apportionments have been paid up to date. I'm convinced that the best way for meeting our obligations is that each month we pay one-twelfth of the total amount due the Conference. You should know your pastor will not be paid until after a check for that one-twelfth of our obligations to the general church has been mailed to the Conference treasurer. The first priority is for missions, not your minister."

That type of coercion appears to be less common today than it was thirty years ago, but it is another approach to making up the deficit. While the members may not be highly motivated to pay all the denominational obligations on schedule, most believe the pastor should be paid on time. If it is necessary to pay the apportionments first, that simply is a hurdle we must surmount to do what is important.

Although some people will question the ethical foundation of what is clearly a coercive approach to church finances, the pragmatists usually display less hesitation.

The Emergency Appeal

Among this range of special appeals the one that is most likely to arouse strong support and only minor opposition is the need to cope with an emergency. The nature of the emergency may vary from relief of the famine in Africa to financial assistance for a family faced with a very expensive operation for a sick child to unanticipated repairs for the heating system to the unexpected opportunity to purchase the property next door at a modest price to an appeal from a local community ministry facing a financial crisis to the family that lost everything when their home was destroyed by fire.

These emergency appeals often produce (a) a generous response from the members and (b) a subsequent debate over whether it would be a better practice to replace these appeals with a contingency item in the congregation's annual budget that could cover unexpected needs. Those in favor of a systematic, orderly, neat, and rational approach to church finances usually favor a larger contingency item in next year's budget. Those more interested in raising larger amounts of money and in a more generous response to emergencies often will endorse the legitimacy of the emergency appeal. They recognize that the term "contingency" is a far less powerful motivating force for raising money than are such words and phrases as fire, famine, suffering child, homeless people, or cold weather.

"Try It, You'll Like It!"

"Last year we proposed adding a half-time person to our staff to work with the youth, and that idea was shot down in the finance committee," explained the person chairing the youth council at St. Paul Church. "Instead of going down that road again, and probably losing again, I'm suggesting we wait until after the first of the year and go directly to our people. Rather than try to get the money in the budget for a part-time youth director, let's have a special offering in February or March and see if we can raise enough money to hire a part-time person to work with the youth for the last six or seven months of the year. That will require less money and when our people see what an improvement that can make in our youth program, I'm sure they'll insist that the position be included in next year's budget."

"But what if we hire someone and the results don't justify making it a permanent position?" questioned a member of the council. "I know several churches that have a youth director, but their program is no better than ours."

"That's a chance we have to take," conceded the person proposing this. "The worst that can happen is we create the position, fill it with a dud, and create a demand that we find a more competent person. At least we'll get the position into next year's budget."

This basic approach to a modest second-mile appeal for a specific need may range from creating a new staff position to raising the money to fund a special short-term event or program to renting a bus. In each case the proponents hope that after people have experienced this, they will institutionalize their support for it.

'Tis better to have done something in the name of love than to have tried nothing in the name of <u>indifference</u>!

—FRIAR TUCK

Response to the Mission Trip

"You are all invited to come see the slides of the mission trip several of our members took while in Brazil last month," urged the pastor one Sunday morning. "As most of you know, six of our members spent ten days working with one of our missionaries in rural Brazil last month. They're back and they have some exciting slides to share with you about their experiences. Please be sure to make this a priority on your calendar."

The following Wednesday evening nearly two-hundred people gathered in the fellowship hall to hear the story and see the slides. After a ninety-minute presentation, which highlighted the poverty of the people in that part of Brazil, a person who had not gone on the trip stood up and proposed, "When I compare what I heard and saw this evening with the affluence we enjoy here in this community, I believe we can help more than we have been doing. Why don't we schedule a special offering for a week from this coming Sunday and ask our people for additional help for our missionary in Brazil?"

The applause that greeted this suggestion convinced everyone that this should be done, even though it violated the standard operating procedures of the finance committee. Eleven days later that special appeal raised an extra $3,600 for missions.

In another congregation the minister returned from a visit to several Puerto Rican congregations and persuaded the people to give the money to purchase a van for one of the churches he had visited.

Similar stories could be told of how a group of teenagers returned from a mission work trip experience and were so motivated by what they had experienced that they conducted a special appeal for missions.

The Annual Catch-up Offering

"Friends, three weeks from today we are asking you to respond to some needs that were not included in the budget we adopted at our annual meeting last January," explained the forty-three-year-old minister one Sunday morning in early April. "In a few days you will receive a letter describing this appeal in more detail, but let me offer a brief introduction. In February our seminary asked if our church could contribute $2,000 to their capital funds campaign. A couple of weeks ago we received a notice from the city of a special assessment for street improvements of $2,800. Just before that we were asked by two of our neighboring churches if we would share in the cost of a seminary intern for the summer to work with the youth from these three congregations. That will cost us $1,200. So, the Board has scheduled a special offering for three weeks from today to cover those three needs that are not included in our budget."

Eighty-five minutes later a young man, who had waited patiently while the pastor greeted the people as they departed, came up to the minister and asked, "Reverend, I've been a member here a little over three years. Every spring, about this same time of the year, you announce a special offering to cover items that were not included in the budget. My question is, Why doesn't someone foresee these and include them in the budget we adopt in January?"

"That's a good question," affirmed the smiling pastor with genuine enthusiasm, "and there are five reasons we do this every April. First there are needs that either could not be foreseen or that were squeezed out of the budget.

"Second, we're just a small church and we have a modest budget. This year the total budget, including missions, comes to a shade under $42,000. As you know, I also serve the Prairie View Church and conduct worship over there at nine-thirty every Sunday morning. We're asking the people here for an extra $6,000. That's about equivalent to 15 percent of our budget. I've served small churches for my entire ministry, and long ago I learned that people in small churches greatly prefer a small budget over a big one, but they're always willing to come up with some extra money if they're convinced there is a genuine need. So, every April, we schedule a special appeal composed of three items. One is to improve the real estate. That's always a winner. Last year, if you remember, we asked for $2,500 to add a second rest room. Now we have a men's rest room and a women's rest room. Before we

If we pitch our appeal
high enough
and soon enough
most congregations
will have time
to get under it!
—FRIAR TUCK

just had the one. Second, we include something for outreach. This year it's the seminary. Last year it was a well in Zaire. A few years ago it was for relief of the famine in Africa. Third, we include something to expand our ministry to our own people and to the general community. Last year it was new hymnals. This year it is a summer youth worker."

"Why April?" inquired the young man.

"Because that's the best time to ask people for money," replied the pastor. "The grass is greener, the birds are singing, the days are getting longer, the flowers are blooming, the death rate is going down, people have paid their income taxes, folks are more optimistic about the future, and everyone is looking forward to a new summer, rather than looking backward."

"You said you had five reasons," came the next question. "What are the other three?"

"The third is that April is a great time to ask people for second-mile giving," replied the pastor. "The fourth is that I am convinced it is good for the church to challenge people, and the fifth is why not?"

A sixth reason, which was not mentioned, is that inflation has made the conventional unified budget obsolete. During the big inflationary wave of 1968–85 a great many congregations that used the concept of a unified budget found themselves short of financial resources. One response was the spring appeal for second-mile giving. This turned out to be a simple and relatively painless means of raising an amount usually equal to 10 to 15 to 20 percent of the budget for specific needs and designated causes. A number of congregations have institutionalized this into an annual April appeal. Others have expanded the concept with a second-mile appeal in late September that also usually produces an amount equivalent to 10 to 15 percent of the budget figure. A common practice is to combine three different needs, one for outreach, one for real estate, and one for program into that annual appeal.

The End of the Tax Year

"Where are you and your family going on vacation after Christmas?" asked one minister of a neighboring pastor.

"Nowhere. I can't afford to be gone that week," came the instant reply.

"Well, we really can't afford it either," replied the first minister, "but my wife teaches in the community college here, and that is vacation time for her as well as for our two teenagers, so we usually go somewhere for three or four days between December 26 and New Year's Day."

"You missed my point," came the clarification. "It is not that I cannot afford to take a brief vacation in late December; it's the congregation that cannot afford my absence that week. While it varies, depending on what day of the week Christmas falls, I always let my members know I'll be in the office for four days near the end of December if they want to talk about some additional charitable contributions before the end of the tax year. I'm available to talk with them either in person or over the telephone. Last year seven members came in to see me personally and another dozen called. Most want to check if our church has some needs that have been overlooked or underfinanced. Others want to get my advice on special mission or outreach needs. One or two usually bring in a check and say, 'Pastor, you indicate where this should go.' A lot of people begin to calculate about December 27 or 28 whether or not they've made all the charitable contributions they planned to make before the end of the tax year. We usually receive an amount equal to 10 percent of our total receipts from member giving during those last five or six days in December.''

"Several months ago you told me you were a strong proponent of only one means of encouraging people to contribute to the church and that was to motivate people only through a sense of being faithful stewards of what God has given them,'' challenged the first minister. "Now you tell me you use the tax laws to motivate giving. How come?''

"Simple,'' came the reply. "A lot of our people wait until near the end of the tax year before they begin to compare their charitable contributions to their total income for the year. I simply make myself available if they want to talk with me about their stewardship. I prefer they contribute to or through our church rather than in response to the pleas for money they receive through the mail in late December. Some of those direct mail appeals are a lot less meritorious than others. If they want to talk about one of those, I'm available to talk with them. That's my style. A friend of mine has a special congregation-wide appeal along the same lines. She sends a letter out to every family several days before the last Sunday in December, and that church receives two offerings on that last Sunday of the year. The first is the regular offering. The second is the catch-up-on-what-you-planned-to-give-this-year appeal. She says the second offering brings in about twice as much as the average Sunday morning offering for the year. That's an extra 4 percent. Another congregation uses a similar approach, and everything received in the catch-up offering goes into the trustees' special fund. The way we do it enables me to place a greater emphasis on outreach, missions, and special needs we could never get into our budget."

The Wish List

The last of these eleven varieties of special appeals appears to be increasingly common. The typical format includes these three steps.

First, every group, staff member, committee, choir, organization, and class are invited to submit a list of what they need that was not included in this year's budget. The list might include a piano for the first- and second-grade Sunday school classroom or hymnals for a new adult Sunday school class or robes for the junior high choir or a folding machine for the church secretary or another volunteer to help with the nursery or additional dishes for the church kitchen or new trees in the yard or an electric hedge trimmer or requests for food for the "Common Pantry" or a rug for a remodeled classroom or money to help resettle an Asian refugee or funds for a special mission project.

Second, these wishes are assembled, usually by an ad hoc committee, into an attractive booklet. Copies are made and given to every family in the congregation.

Third, people are invited to respond to these wishes. The responses may include money, canned food, a secondhand piano, office equipment, and a variety of other goods and services.

The purpose is to make an annual systematic appeal to bring together needs and resources.

The Common Threads

These eleven varieties of special appeals share several common elements. The first, and perhaps the most obvious, is that each one is based on the assumption that the best way of securing additional resources is to ask for them.

Second, some people respond to and others will ignore a particular appeal. One reason for the variety is to increase the chances that every member will find at least one of these special appeals to be attractive. No matter when a special appeal is scheduled, that almost always turns out to be a good time for some people to respond affirmatively while it is an inconvenient time for others.

Third, each one is designed to supplement the regular channels for mobilizing resources.

Fourth, most of these appeals focus on specifics that are visual, attractive, and comprehensible. Most people easily comprehend the need to help that visiting choir pay their travel expenses or the need for a piano in a children's classroom or the need to make sure all bills are paid or the needs of a missionary in a poverty-stricken part of the world. It is more difficult for many people to be motivated by the goal of underwriting a $94,000 church budget.

Fifth, each of these special appeals conveys to the potential contributor that you can know for sure where and how your contribution will be used. The concept of designated giving is a powerful motivating force. It appears to be increasingly powerful with the continued erosion of denominational loyalties, the growing distrust of people in official positions of authority, and the rise in the level of formal education of the general public.

Finally, each of these special appeals is based on the assumption that the churches have done a better job teaching stewardship than many leaders are willing to concede, that Christians do have generous hearts, and that when asked, people will respond. The results of these and similar minor special appeals suggest this is a valid assumption.

CHAPTER FIVE

Bequests and Memorials

Sixty years ago common synonyms for the word "poor" were "elderly" or "widowed." Today the two most common synonyms in the United States for "poor" are "child" and "single-parent mother."

During the first four decades of this century many men made a living by going door to door to collect the weekly premiums on burial insurance. Tens of thousands of urban residents worried that their death might create a financial burden for their children, so they took out a life insurance policy that cost a dime or a quarter a week and promised enough money to insure them a decent burial when they died.

Among the many changes that have occurred in American society since the 1930s three stand out that influence the emphasis in this chapter. First, in actual dollars per capita, personal income in the United States climbed from $595 in 1940 to nearly $14,000 in 1987. After allowing for inflation the real increase was from $595 in 1940 to $1,550 in 1987 using the Consumer Price Index to adjust for inflation. In other words, per capita personal income nearly tripled after allowing for the impact of inflation. On a per capita basis the average income of all Americans sixty-five years old and over is now slightly higher than that for the rest of the population.

Second, the private net worth of all Americans more than tripled between 1945 and 1985; again that increase has been adjusted for inflation. Approximately three-quarters of the accumulated private wealth in the

United States is held by individuals aged 50 and over. Americans aged 65 and over account for 13 percent of the nation's population, but hold 40 percent of the accumulated wealth.

Third, if the life expectancy rates of 1970 still prevailed, well over 2 million Americans, aged 65 and over, who are now alive would be dead. The past two decades have brought medical advances that have enabled people to survive what formerly were terminal illnesses or fatal accidents.

This combination of sharply increased incomes, vast increases in accumulated private wealth, and longer life expectancy has created a new generation of relatively affluent mature adults. This change, of course, has been facilitated by the increase in Social Security payments (the average Social Security payment to retired couples nearly quadrupled between 1970 and 1986 while the Consumer Price Index climbed from 116 to 335), the proliferation of private pensions, the favorable pension benefits received by retired governmental employees, the widespread pattern of home ownership, and the sharp increases in the the price of real estate.

The Fruits of Affluence

One result of these changes, along with the birth dearth of the 1970s, has been an aging of the American population. The median age has climbed from 27.9 years in 1970 to 31.8 in 1987. Another result, which is the product of many other factors, is the aging of the membership of several of the "old-line" Protestant denominations, most notably the Christian Church (Disciples of Christ), The United Methodist Church, the Presbyterian Church (U.S.A.), and The United Church of Christ.

A third result is the number of bequests received by congregations affiliated with the old-line Protestant denominations has at least tripled since 1965. A fourth result is that if an attractive cause is identified, the contributions to memorial funds frequently include checks for $25, $50, $100, $200, $500, or even $1,000.

Three Questions

These changes raise three policy questions on church finances. First, do you want to encourage people to remember your church in their will? Do you want to encourage substantial memorial gifts?

Neither is difficult. A growing number of churches twice a year schedule one Sunday when the theme for the day is the Christian view of death. This is the theme of the sermon and a topic in one or more Sunday school classes. During the afternoon three or four discussion groups or forums may be offered, one of which lifts up the benefits of everyone having a will for their survivors (nearly one-half of all church members die before having prepared a will). The possibility of tithing one's estate or of leaving a specific bequest to the church is discussed. Other congregations mail every member a brochure encouraging this concept. This also can be a subject for discussion in adult Sunday school classes or in the women's organization. In 1969 one congregation

posted on the walls of the corridor leading into the educational wing a twelve-foot long sign that read,

OUR TWENTY-YEAR PLAN FOR IMPROVE-MENT OF OUR CHURCH HOME

Under that long sign were sketches of a dozen proposed improvements to the property with the estimated cost attached to each one. Fifteen years later the twenty-year plan had been completely implemented and over one-half of the cost came from bequests and memorial gifts.

A parallel component of this effort to give a large role to memorial gifts can be presented in the question, What do you prefer for a memorial when you die? Members are encouraged to fill out a form answering this and several other questions concerning their death and that form is placed in the church files. The questions may include disposal of the remains, hymns to be sung at the memorial service, persons to be notified, and a variety of other questions that can best be answered in advance. This can be a highly desirable sheet of information for the immediate family when someone dies.

In one congregation a lifelong member decided she would like to have people contribute toward the purchase of a church-owned van when she died. She did not keep her dream secret. Within a week after her death, memorial gifts had been received to cover the full cost of the van plus a year's insurance and maintenance. The more widely supported the cause and the more expensive the memorial, the larger the amounts given as memorials.

Obviously bequests and memorials will be a bigger factor in the financial base in the long-established congregation that includes many mature members than in the new congregation composed largely of people born after 1950.

What If It Works?

The second, and by far the most serious question can result from the success of an effort to encourage people to remember the church in their wills and/or to expand the role of memorial gifts. It is not healthy for congregations to be living off the gifts of the dead! The nature of this problem can be exacerbated when the majority of the living leaders fail to see that as a problem, but rather perceive it as an asset.

In addition, it is not unusual for members to reduce their level of giving in response to what they perceive as a well-endowed congregation or to encourage the leaders to rely more heavily on the endowment fund to pay the current bills. "Why should I increase my giving when the annual report shows this congregation has over a half million dollars invested in stocks and bonds?"

Do you want, as a matter of policy, to encourage the possibility your congregation will become excessively dependent on bequests and memorials?

One Alternative

If the answer to that second policy question is in the negative, that raises the last of these three policy

Just one more piece of evidence that there's life after death!

—FRIAR TUCK.

questions. Do you want to create a separate trust or foundation, with its own officers and reporting system, that will have the full jurisdiction over bequests and memorial gifts? Many congregations have created their own foundation, some as a separate legal corporation, others under the corporate umbrella of the congregation's articles of incorporation. These foundations offer several benefits.

First this arrangement normally requires a separate set of trustees for the foundation, a majority of whom do not hold any other policy-making office while serving in this role. (Ideally none will be policy-makers while serving as trustees of the foundation.) The foundation trustees soon learn the number one responsibility of any foundation trustee is to keep other people's hands off that money and, if they serve six- or nine-year terms, they become highly skilled at this. This "arms length" relationship reduces the chances the congregation will become dependent on the foundation to meet expenses that should be covered by living donors.

Second, and perhaps most important, the foundation or trust eliminates the temptation of the finance committee to act in an irresponsible manner. Since it receives and administers bequests, special gifts, and memorials, that keeps those items off the congregational agenda and enables the boards and committees of the congregation to concentrate on ministry, mission, stewardship, and outreach.

Third, if the foundation is a separate legal entity, it is easier to establish and to maintain restrictions on the use of these funds. Frequently the foundation allocates most of the income to missions, scholarships, and to matching grants for launching new ministries and/or maintenance of the property. If the building needs a new roof, the foundation may contribute one dollar for each two dollars given by members. This arrangement makes it very difficult for the finance committee to "borrow" from the endowment funds to offset the summer slump or to pay for unexpected repairs to the building that are not covered by the budget.

Fourth, since these investments are not controlled by the finance committee or the congregation directly, that largely eliminates the temptation of "why should I increase my giving when this church has hundreds of thousands of dollars in the bank? Why not spend that before asking the members to give more?" When the money is controlled by the foundation and the reporting is outside the normal congregational reporting system, that excuse is eliminated.

Fifth, the existence of the foundation can relieve some of the guilt mature members feel about their level of giving. A frequent comment resembles this, "My husband left me comparatively well off when he died, and I'm grateful. I suppose I could and should give more to the church, but I'm eighty-one and I don't know how much longer I'll live. I don't want to go on welfare or have to be dependent on my children. If I knew I would die before I'm eighty-five, I could make a more generous contribution to the church. But what if I live to be ninety-seven as my sister did? I don't want to outlive my money. I really don't know what to do."

One response could be for this widow to include in her will the foundation to receive a proportion of her estate when she dies. Her guilt would be relieved and she could die feeling she had been a good and faithful steward.

Sixth, the responsible policies and actions of the foundation trustees can encourage members to remember the foundation in their wills, secure in the knowledge that the foundation can be depended on to function as a responsible steward of the future bequests.

Seventh, the foundation can encourage a more generous response to mission giving by the members. A common example is that when the special denominational appeal is made for missions, the foundation offers to match, on a two-for-one basis, every dollar the members give above the apportionment or goal or quota for that appeal.

In summary, endowment funds directly controlled by the finance committee and policy-makers of that congregation often tend to have a blighting impact on the stewardship, vitality, perspective, and value system of that congregation. By contrast, foundations tend to have a creative, challenging, and helpful influence. Normally, the trustees of the foundation are elected at a congregational meeting, but in some states this can be a self-perpetuating board in which replacements are nominated and elected by the foundation trustees. That is a less significant variable than avoiding conflict-of-interest problems.

Finally, a response is due those who ask, "Instead of encouraging members to leave part of their estate to the church, wouldn't it be better to encourage them to leave that money to a denominational foundation?" That probably would be a better arrangement. The difficulty is that a shrinking proportion of church members display a denominational loyalty that would motivate them to do this. Frequently, that bequest will go either to that congregation or to a person or cause unrelated to that denomination.

CHAPTER SIX

User Fees

"You want to charge seven-year-old kids to attend our vacation Bible school?" challenged an incredulous Clint Miller. "When my wife taught in the vacation Bible school twenty years ago, we went around the neighborhood begging kids to come. Now, you tell me, you plan to charge each kid five bucks to attend for two weeks! What is this? A scheme to discontinue vacation Bible school!"

*　　*　　*

The first turnpike, a road which a traveler must pay a fee or toll to use, probably was a Persian military road between Babylon and Syria constructed nearly 4,000 years ago. The first turnpike in the United States was constructed in Virginia in 1785, but the sixty-two-mile turnpike connecting Philadelphia to Lancaster completed twelve years later became far more famous since it was the first one to be granted a charter. For over a century, from 1820 to 1935, the concept was largely abandoned in the United States, but the past fifty years have brought the construction of dozens of new toll roads and toll bridges. Several toll roads are included in the Interstate Highway System.

*　　*　　*

"The total cost will be $1,675, exclusive of the caterer," summarized Mrs. Evelyn Gardiner, wedding consultant at First Church as she concluded a two-hour planning session with Vicki Stevens and Vicki's parents one Saturday morning in early May. Seven years earlier, Vicki had moved to this city to work for the largest bank in the state. A few years later Vicki had met and fallen in love with the man she planned to marry this next August. While Vicki attended Sunday morning worship at First Church a dozen or more Sundays a year, she had not transferred her membership. Her parents had hoped Vicki would be married in their church 740 miles away where both Mr. and Mrs. Stevens were active members, but Vicki had explained, "All my close friends of today and all Jack's friends and relatives live where I work, not where I grew up. It would be so much simpler for you two to come 740 miles for the wedding than for everyone else to travel that distance."

So, on this beautiful weekend in May Vicki's parents had flown over to visit their daughter and to arrange the final details of the wedding.

Earlier, when Vicki and Jack had stopped in to see the senior minister, he had agreed to officiate at the wedding and asked to meet with the two of them together for an hour on two different evenings for premarital counseling. He added, "Just so there is no misunderstanding, I do not come to wedding rehearsals nor do I make the arrangements for all the details. Our staff includes a part-time wedding consultant, Mrs. Evelyn Gardiner, and you'll have to make an appointment to talk with her about the details. I have put you on the church calendar for 4:00 P.M. on the second Saturday in August, and the church is reserved for you for that time. We do have another wedding at one o'clock that afternoon, but that should not be a problem."

As Mrs. Gardiner met with Vicki and her parents that

Saturday morning, she learned the Stevens had planned to have a reception followed by a catered meal for sixty people in the fellowship hall at First Church. "We have a list of five caterers who have been approved by our trustees to use our building," explained Mrs. Gardiner. "You may pick the one you wish and make the arrangements directly, or I will do that for you if you prefer." After a three-minute whispered conversation the Stevens decided to entrust Mrs. Gardiner with that responsibility.

Mrs. Gardiner explained that Vicki should meet with her, not with the senior minister, in planning the Friday night wedding rehearsal and in arranging for the flowers and other decorations. At the end of this conversation Mrs. Gardiner went over the fee schedule on a line-by-line basis with the Stevens and explained that the $1675 total included her fee, the use of the building including the cost of the air conditioning, the honoraria for the organist, soloist, pastor, and custodian, the cost of laundering the tablecloths and napkins, and the fee for the caterer's use of the kitchen. It was agreed the caterer would send a separate bill directly to the Stevens.

As they walked out to the car, Mr. Stevens commented to his wife, "That's not as bad as what it cost us when Beth was married two years ago and we had the reception and dinner at the country club. We only had fifty people for the dinner, and that whole deal cost us nearly $1,000 more than this will."

"I told you, Dad," explained Vicki, "it would be better for me to be married here than back home."

*   *   *

In recent years, when voters failed to approve an increase in the tax levy, dozens of public high schools

instituted a fee system to charge teenagers who choose
to participate in athletics, band, and other extracurricu-
lar activities. The fee is charged only to those who elect
to participate in that particular sport or activity.

*   *   *

"We either will have to close the school or begin to
charge tuition for children of members," declared
Clarence Schmidt, a member of the parish education
board at St. John Lutheran Church. "We bought some
time three years ago when we raised the tuition for
children from nonmember families from $700 to $1,100
a year, but four-fifths of our enrollment comes from
member families. We simply cannot continue to ask the
teachers to subsidize this school by working for such
low salaries!"

"We started this school in 1926, and it has always
been tuition-free for members," recalled Howard
Kaiser. "I went to school here from 1931 to 1939, and it
seems to me if we could run it without tuition in the
depths of the Great Depression, we should be able to do
so today. I'm opposed to charging our own people for
sending their kids to our school."

Fourteen months and seventeen meetings later the
leaders at St. John Lutheran Church adopted a tuition
schedule of $1,400 for the first child from any family,
$1,000 for the second, and $800 for each additional child
from that same family enrolled that same year. The fee
schedule included a $300 per child discount for children
from member families.

*   *   *

Many Christian pastoral counselors insist their
clients pay a fee, even if it is less than full cost. One

reason for charging a fee is that it is a means of increasing the level of the client's commitment to the process.

*   *   *

The announcement on the bulletin board at Trinity Church invited people to enroll in a new Bible study program that would meet for two hours on Tuesday evenings during the next eight months. "The cost for the thirty-two sessions is $45. That includes the study manual, refreshments, and a modest honorarium for the instructor."

*   *   *

These seven illustrations introduce what in recent years may be the most rapidly growing source of funds for churches. These seven illustrations also introduce one of the most significant public policy debates of our era.

From the churches' perspective the subject is the user fee. The consumer of a service is expected to pay at least part, if not all, of the cost of providing that service. It is not unusual today to find congregations in which more than one-third of the total annual income of that parish comes from user fees.

It also must be noted that in a substantial number of congregations the idea of user fees is repugnant to many leaders, including a fair share of the clergy. They find any proposal to accept a fee for the Christian day school or to ask any outsider to pay for use of a meeting room in the building to be absolutely contrary to their value system. Others are comfortable with the concept of user fees for certain programs and services, but not for others.

...is an idea that's hard to swallow until we see how much we have to cough up to pay our bills!

USER FEES...

—FRIAR TUCK

The public policy debate includes at least two major themes. The more highly visible is the trend by governmental organizations to charge fees for special services and programs. The range of these include the admission fee to state and national parks, the fee to go swimming in the municipal pool, the fee charged farmers in the West for irrigation water, the fee charged the subdivider who wants to turn a farm into a subdivision with 237 lots, the charges paid by people on Medicare and Medicaid, the continued construction of toll roads and toll bridges, and the decision to require the Government Printing Office to charge full cost for all the publications that formerly were heavily subsidized.

Who Receives the Subsidy?

The other and far more controversial side of that public policy debate concerns subsidies. Traditionally, the public subsidies have gone to the provider of the service, not the recipient. Thus the public school system, the municipal hospital, the local housing authority, the Army Corps of Engineers, and scores of other agencies receive tax funds to provide subsidized services to consumers. Back in the 1960s a growing number of religious organizations began to be recipients of public funds to help pay the cost of providing subsidized housing for low income families or to provide counseling, educational programs, job training, and other services.

One of the first big breaks in that tradition of subsidizing the producer of services, rather than the consumer, came with the G.I. Bill of World War II that offered veterans a financial subsidy for their education.

What has turned out to be an even bigger break with tradition came with the Higher Education Act of 1965, and especially with the revision signed into law in July of 1972 by President Richard M. Nixon.[1] The 1972 act included a provision introduced by Senator Claiborne Pell (D. Rhode Island) called basic educational grants. The 1972 senate bill provided scholarships of up to $1,400 for college students. The innovative feature that the Senate added to the legislation is that this subsidy would be allocated to the *consumer*, rather than to the *producer*, of educational services.

This proposal by Senator Pell aroused strong opposition from many colleges and universities, including Harvard, Holy Cross, Boston University, MIT, the University of Rhode Island, and Wellesley. When the subject of federal aid to higher education was being discussed at a meeting held at Boston College in December 1971, Senator Pell stated the issue clearly to the representatives of eastern schools when he asked, "Will federal policy be focused on people, on youngsters and their needs, or will it focus primarily on the needs of institutions?"

Since Senator Pell was chairman of the Senate Labor and Public Welfare subcommittee and the author of the basic educational grant provision, his views deserved and received serious consideration.

The opposite point of view, and the one supported by many representatives of colleges and universities, was stated in the House version of the bill supported by Congresswoman Edith Green of Oregon who was chairwoman of the House Education Committee. The Green bill called for granting the subsidies to the producers rather than to the consumers of educational services. This was defeated.

While this has turned out to be one of the most significant efforts to change the philosophy underlying the granting of subsidies, it was not the first. A few of the federal subsidies to agriculture have been changed over the years to subsidize the consumers of food rather than the long line of producers. The most highly visible current example is food stamps. (One of the most controversial public questions in Western Europe, Canada, and the United States today is over whether governmental subsidies for food should go to the producers or to the consumers.)

The Housing Act of 1968 began the process of changing the system of federal subsidies for housing. Sections 235 and 236 of that Act provided subsidies to the consumers of housing services. This contrasts with thirty-five years of public housing and with Sections 202, 221, 231, and other earlier subsidies that subsidized the producer of housing for low income persons.

Other examples of this change in philosophy include Medicare, Social Security, Aid to Dependent Children, and burial benefits for veterans. In each case the subsidy is directed at the consumer of services, rather than at the producer of services.

What would happen if the churches made a parallel shift in the policies underlying denominational grants and subsidies?

It would mean that instead of annual grants to denominational theological seminaries, the churches might provide vouchers of $5,000 to $10,000 each to seminary students. The students would pick the seminary they wanted to attend and turn the voucher in toward their bill for tuition, books, room, and board.

It would mean that instead of subsidizing the operation of a church camp, the regional judicatory might divide that amount of money among the prospective campers and issue vouchers good for $25 or $50 or $100 per camper and the camper could pick his or her camp from a list of approved operations.

It would mean that instead of an annual subsidy of perhaps $50,000 to a home for the elderly, the regional judicatory would offer a series of "scholarships" to elderly persons in need of decent housing.

It would mean that instead of the $25,000 annual subsidy to the school of nursing run by the denominational hospital, there might be a dozen $2,000 scholarships to prospective students in financial need.

It would mean that instead of providing "free" consultative services by denominational staff to congregations, the denomination would pay only one-fourth to perhaps one-half of the cost to a congregation involved in securing an outside consultant.

It would mean that instead of subsidizing the producers of continuing education programs for ministers, the denomination would offer vouchers to ministers each year. The pastors could pick the place and type of continuing education they believed they needed and, if necessary, save up their vouchers for two or three or four years to pay the cost. (This, of course, has been happening for many years now.)

It would mean that instead of subsidizing the operation of a community center in a poverty neighborhood, the denomination would make funds available to be used by the consumers of these services, and they could buy the services they felt they needed from whatever source was available.

For some denominational leaders the most threatening product of this change in how subsidies are granted would be in the system for supporting missionaries. Here again that change already is well under way. In the 1950s the dominant pattern was for congregations to send money to denominational missionary boards. These national denominational agencies would recruit, examine, screen, train, and send missionaries to various parts of the globe. The subsidy went from the congregation to the denominational missions board to the missionary. During the past three decades a rapidly growing proportion of missionaries is being supported directly by the churches, rather than through a national missions board. The next step, which already is being implemented, is for American congregations to send their money directly to a Christian organization in some other part of the world so the consumers of that staff person's time and talents can recruit that person directly rather than receive a missionary chosen by someone else in another country.

The dominant pattern in American Protestantism, however, is still to grant subsidies to the producer of services, rather than to the consumers. As pointed out earlier, the list of exceptions is growing, but it is still a relatively short list. In addition to the financial support of missionaries, the funding for the continuing education of pastors, and scholarships for seminarians, this list includes a limited number of scholarships to foreign students or to persons from minority groups, a few churches that make direct appropriations to retired ministers rather than channeling these grants through a denominational pension board, and some forms of salary supplement that are directed to the congregation rather than to the pastor.

In general, however, the churches continue to make their annual appropriations of money in a form that subsidizes the producer of the services rather than the consumer. Examples of this include the annual appropriations to church-related hospitals, homes, community centers, colleges, seminaries, camps, denominational periodicals, pension boards, regional staff, councils of churches, continuing education programs, cooperative ministries, and supplemental income for pastors of small congregations.

A few denominations and a rapidly growing number of congregations are now making grants directly to the poor, the oppressed, the downtrodden, the homeless, the hungry, the ill, the indigent, and the victims of disasters rather than to the agencies that traditionally have existed to provide services for these people.

What Are the Implications?

When the President signed the 1972 aid to higher education bill, it was hailed as the most important piece of legislation affecting higher education since the Morrill Act (which in 1862 established a network of land grant colleges and universities). It also is another step in a major trend in how services will be financed. If this concept of subsidizing the consumer rather than the producer of services continues to spread, what will be the implications?

As with every other change, this one has price tags attached to it. Perhaps the largest is the problem of quality control. This turned out to be a major issue in efforts to direct the subsidy to the low income consumer of housing under Sections 235 and 236 of the Housing Act of 1968. It also is a problem in Medicare and in several forms of public assistance. In each case there has been difficulty in policing the program to ensure that the consumer gets full value for each dollar expended.

Several denominational leaders contend this has

become a major problem in continuing education for the clergy. Some programs clearly are of a higher quality than others.

What will be the means for ensuring quality control when vouchers for housing for low income families become more common?

At their 1986 conference in South Carolina the governors from the various states adopted a position paper advocating that parents, who now had a choice where their children attend nursery school or college, also be given the freedom of choice in determining where their children will attend elementary school and high school. Public opinion surveys indicate a growing number of black parents support proposals for vouchers that will enable them to pick the school of their choice. That, of course, would be consistent with the basic concept of subsidizing the consumer, rather than the producer, of services.

Advocates of this position also contend that it will be more economical as competition will result in lower costs. They also argue that the freedom of choice will take care of the quality control problem. In many communities, however, the public schools cannot compete with the private schools on the basis of costs and quality and that fact will slow adoption of the governor's proposal. Minnesota is the first state to adopt the voucher system for public school children.

Closely related to this is the problem of accountability. When the grants are directed to the producer of services, rather than to the consumer, it is far easier to maintain adequate lines of accountability. An outstanding recent illustration of this is described by Richard W. Poston in *The Gang and the Establishment*, an account of how "consumer oriented" grants to street gangs to attack ghetto problems turned into a fascinating "hustle" of the establishment by gangs.[2]

On the other side of the ledger are three important considerations. The first is that this approach is consistent with the growing anti-bureaucratic sentiment of the day. The second is that subsidizing the consumer directly is one means of making the producers of services pay more careful attention to costs. When the subsidy comes directly to the producer of services, the temptation of the administrator of the agency is to focus more attention on raising money than on keeping costs down.

In our time, god seems to be working for the independence of individuals instead of the security of institutions!

Far more important in the long run, however, is the mounting evidence that this trend toward subsidizing the consumer rather than the producer of services is compatible with the growing demand for freedom of choice, with the rapidly accelerating trend toward granting the client a greater voice in the making of the policies that affect his or her destiny and in the dawning realization that people no longer can be managed as they could be ten or twenty or fifty years ago.

Perhaps most fundamental of all, the 1972 Aid to Higher Education Act raises for the churches the question, Will the policies of religious organizations be focused on the people and their needs or on the needs of institutions?

Why Raise It Here?

Five reasons stand out for discussing this change in public policy under the general subject of user fees. The first is that frequently church policies follow changes in public policy. Obvious examples include the efforts to racially integrate the churches, granting women the right to hold influential offices in both congregations and denominational agencies, and a variety of efforts by the church to provide subsidized housing for low income families and the elderly. Earlier examples include the founding of church-sponsored orphanages following Abraham Lincoln's second inaugural address of 1865 and the support by the churches for the American position in World War I.

Second, and perhaps least visible, is the shift in the mix of the churches in American Protestantism. From 1607 until the 1950s most of the Christian congregations in the United States, and nearly all of the large churches, were affiliated with one of a dozen or so denominations. During the past three decades a growing proportion of all Protestant congregations and a majority of the congregations averaging over 3,000 at worship do not carry any denominational affiliation.

For these congregations the easy and natural course of action is to subsidize the consumers of services directly, rather than to send money to the producers of services. Rather than support a theological seminary, they will offer scholarships to members who pick the school they want to attend. Rather than send money to a mission board, they support missionaries directly. Rather than support a denominational agency that publishes Sunday school materials, they will pay full cost to an independent publisher. Rather than send money to a denominational social services agency, they will provide direct services to those in need of emergency help.

Third, the continued erosion of denominational loyalty over the past three or four decades often means it is easier to raise money designated for a particular cause or person than it is to motivate members to contribute to the support of a faceless bureaucracy.

Fourth, and from the perspective of many readers the most important reason for raising this issue concerns congregational policies on the expansion of the program.

One example is the response to the demand for "high quality, low cost child care." Should your congregation create a child care program for the all-day care of young children of mothers employed outside the home? If yes, should user fees be charged to cover full costs? Or should your congregation subsidize the child care operation? Or should you offer grants to parents who cannot afford the full cost? If you decide to subsidize the consumer, rather than the producer of this service, why start a child care center? Why not simply use those funds to provide grants to needy parents and let the parents choose the child care facility that comes closest to meeting their needs in terms of location or quality or style? Or is the choice of subsidizing the producer of the services based on a desire to control the program? Or to be able to take credit for offering it?

If the primary point of concern is either (a) helping the low income working parent and/or (b) improving the quality of child care for these parents, one alternative would be to make financial grants to needy parents and let them choose the type and location of child care they prefer, which might include payments to a live-in relative. A second alternative would be to offer subsidized training for those women who are offering child care in their homes. The training could be designed to improve the competence of the care given. A third alternative would be vouchers to parents who could direct these funds to improve the quality of the facilities used by mothers offering child care in their homes. This might, for example, include fencing a play area or providing more outdoor equipment. Inasmuch as many low income working parents cannot afford or prefer not to utilize institutional child care, it may be wise to offer them choices. The simplest way to do that would be to subsidize the consumer, rather than the producer of services.

The fifth reason for raising this policy question brings us back to the central issue of user fees. Most churches that do rely on user fees charge less than full cost. This generalization applies to the fees charged for vacation Bible school or the fees charged the youth going on a ski trip or the fees charged by the pastoral counseling center at the church or the tuition for the Christian Day School or for participation in that Tuesday evening Bible study group or the fee for weddings.

If your congregation decides to go down the road of greater reliance on use fees, sooner or later you will be faced with the question of charging full cost or only partial cost. If the decision is to charge partial cost, that means subsidizing the producer of the services. That means running counter to the trend of recent decades.

The most frequently heard argument in favor of subsidizing the producer of services is, "But if we charged people the full cost of what it costs us to provide all-day child care, we wouldn't have anyone using our service." The words "all-day child care" in that sentence can be replaced by "weekday nursery school" or "high school youth program" or "adult day care center" or "Sunday school" or "Mothers' Morning Out" or "weekday adult Bible study groups" or "Tuesday lunches for senior citizens" or "Christian Day School" or "pastoral counseling services" or a variety of other programs. This argument suggests that the churches must depend on the fact that the service or program is offered below cost, rather than on the quality or merit of the program to attract participants. If that is true, that can be interpreted as a very disturbing evaluation.

What Should We Do?

The formulation of a congregational policy on the subject of user fees may be the most perplexing issue raised in this book. For most congregations a greater reliance on user fees represents a sharp break with tradition. For most of American Protestantism the tradition has been to subsidize the producer of the services rather than to charge user fees. Some people may object to a greater emphasis on user fees on the grounds that it is close to certain practices in Catholicism. Others may raise questions about "works righteousness." At least a few will contend the concept of user fees is incompatible with the Christian view of God's unbounded love.

On the other side will be heard arguments such as, "If we don't recover at least part of the cost through user fees, we will not be able to offer that program," or "Let's use market forces to help us set priorities," or "Let the people who want it pay for it," or "People take a greater interest in that which they help pay for," or "If people are asked to help pay for it, they will accept more responsibility for their own participation."

The most common response to this divisive issue is to charge user fees to recover part of the costs of new programs, but not to charge for long-established programs. Thus the parents of the three-year-old child are not expected to pay a fee when that child comes to Sunday school, but a fee is charged for participation in the church-operated Tuesday–Thursday nursery

school that opened last year. A fee is not charged for
participation in the children's choir, but a fee is charged
for participation in the music encounter program for
young children that begins next week. Never underestimate the power of precedent!

Some congregations resolve this issue by charging
user fees for what are identified as "community service
programs" (the pastoral counseling center, the weekday early childhood development center, weekday
child care, divorce recovery programs), but do not
charge for what are considered to be "ministries of our
church" (worship, Sunday school, Bible study, counseling, the youth program, weddings, funerals, bap-
tisms, pastoral care). Many congregations do charge
nonmembers a fee for services that are available to
members without any direct charge.

As the services and programs offered by churches
increase, the issue of competition may be raised.
Should the churches offer new programs that parallel
what is now offered by private profit-making business
or by public agencies? Should the churches offer
birthday planning services including the after-school
birthday party at the church for the nine-year-old child
of working parents? Should the churches offer weekday nursery schools in competition with public and/or
private nursery schools? Should the church urge brides
to utilize the services of a member who is a bridal
consultant? Should the churches offer music lessons for
children? For adults? Should the churches schedule
supervised after-school activities for children whose
parents do not get home from work until 6:00 P.M.?
Should the churches offer aerobic dance classes when
the exercise classes at the YMCA or YWCA are not
filled? Should the churches serve subsidized meals in
competition with tax-paying restaurants? Should the
churches compete with the local community college in

offering evening classes for adults? Should the churches compete with the travel agency in offering all-day or overnight excursions for mature adults? Should the churches offer subsidized music lessons when the private music teachers in this community cannot make a living?

One response is, "The churches should never compete with private profit-making businesses!" Another is, "Why not?" A third is, "Only if these programs and ministries include what is clearly a Christian dimension and emphatically proclaim the gospel." A fourth is, "Only if it pays its own way. We cannot afford to subsidize it." What is your response as you formulate the policy on user fees for your church?

For some the most disturbing question raises a highly subjective issue. What proportion of a congregation's total receipts should come from user fees? Will it undercut the health and vitality of that congregation if one-third or more of all receipts come from user fees paid by nonmembers? Does the evidence suggest that can become a problem? At least five congregations closed within months after the enforcement of state regulations forced these congregations to terminate weekday programming that produced more than one-half of each congregation's total income from user fees. How dependent should a congregation become on user fees? Should user fees be seen as strictly a limited source of supplemental funds? Or is it acceptable for user fees to help meet the mortgage payments on the proposed new building we plan to construct?

Finally, and for some readers the most critical questions concern role and purpose. If we turn to user fees as a means of expanding our financial base, will that influence the operational definition of our role as a church? Will that influence our response to God's call to be a faithful and obedient servant? How will a greater dependence on user fees affect the way we set our priorities?

Notes

1. For a discussion of the changes in federal policy on aid to higher education see Francis Keppel, "The Higher Education Acts Contrasted, 1965–1986. Has Federal Policy Come of Age?" *Harvard Educational Review*, vol. 57, February, 1987, pp. 49-67.
2. Richard W. Poston, *The Gang and the Establishment* (New York: Harper & Row, 1971).

CHAPTER SEVEN

Twenty-six Other Approaches

The newly arrived pastor had decided one of his priorities in this small town pastorate would be to call on every shut-in as soon as possible. Six days after he had arrived, he called on Nelda Swann, an eighty-six-year-old lifelong member of this parish. Nelda had been widowed for twenty-three years, but was still able to live alone although she had great difficulty climbing stairs. As he came to the close of this get-acquainted visit, the new minister asked Nelda to join him in prayer. Following this, he stood up to leave. As he began to thank Nelda for what truly had been an interesting visit, she interrupted his good-bye speech.

The Angel

"Reverend, sit back down," she began. "There's one more thing you should know. My late husband and I were both products of the Great Depression. We both learned how to save money, but neither of us ever was very good at spending it. The result is I'm comfortably well off today. Oh, I'm not rich but I have more than enough to live comfortably if I don't live too long. If you ever need money for some special project or program and you can't get it out of that bunch of cheap skates who run the church's finances, you come to me. I'll help you. I won't give you all you need, but I'll give you half of it. You can use that half to motivate some of the rest of the folks to match what I give."

"That's most generous of you," interrupted the surprised pastor who was overwhelmed by what for him was an unprecedented experience.

"There are only three restrictions on this offer," added Nelda. "Don't come too often, don't ask for too much, and don't ever tell anyone the source of this money. The only person who should know about this besides you and me is the church's financial secretary. She already knows, but she also knows how to keep secrets."

On more than a dozen occasions during the next eight years before Nelda's death this pastor went to talk with her about what he considered to be a great idea or an unmet need or a potential new ministry. Each visit produced a promise that within twenty-four hours she would send a check to the financial secretary for one-half of the amount needed. The amounts ranged from $300 to $6,000. Each time the minister was successful in using this anonymous contribution as the basis for securing the rest of the needed funds.

Two days following Nelda's funeral, another mature member called the pastor and asked him to drop by for a visit. Five minutes after the pastor's arrival, the member said, "Don't ask me what I know or how I know it, but I'm ready to take Nelda's place as your angel. From now on you come to me when you need a down payment on a good idea."

One moral of that story is that it is difficult to keep secrets in small town America. A second is that one means of expanding the financial base of your congregation is to find an angel who will provide the incentive gift that motivates others to help fund special needs.

Garage Sales: God's way of redistributing the wealth by recycling our junk!
—FRIAR TUCK

Other alternatives for expanding that financial base can be found by listening in to what was said at a workshop on church finances that brought together people from more than a dozen different denominational backgrounds. The period after lunch on the second day was devoted to a "show and tell" session in which the participants shared some of their success stories from back home. Several of these are summarized here.

The Garage Sale

"Our church has a garage sale every spring and fall," explained a leader from an eleven-year-old congregation. "We have a high turnover in our membership, so five years ago our trustees decided to sponsor a rummage sale twice a year. We don't have a sanctuary,

just one big multi-purpose room and on two Saturdays
every year that is filled with stuff people want to sell.
Anything that's not sold by noon is marked down to
half price. The owner gets half of what the item brings,
and the other half goes into our building fund. We're in
desperate need of more educational space, but we still
have four years to go before our mortgage on our first
unit will be paid off. Our garage sales bring in between
$1,500 and $3,000 each time, and the money goes into
the fund for our next building program. With the
interest that's been earned, we now have $45,000 in that
fund. In addition, we help people find secondhand
toys, furniture, children's clothing, and lots of other
stuff they can use at a reasonable price. It's true that one
person's junk can become someone else's treasure."

How Many Financial Statements?

"Our church has always sent out quarterly financial
statements to all the members to help them see how
much they have given to date," explained the
chairperson of the finance committee of a sixty-eight-
year-old congregation. "Since we use the calendar year
as our fiscal year, these were mailed about the middle of
April, July, October, and early January. The fourth one
gave people information they needed to make out their
income tax returns. Several years ago we got a new
member of our committee who persuaded us we should
send five a year. She pointed out the fourth one mailed
in January arrived after the end of the church year and
after the end of the tax year. That meant if anyone had
given less than they planned to give, it was too late to
correct that for that church year or for the tax year. So
we now mail a fourth statement in early December
that reports total contributions for the first

forty-nine weeks of the year. The Sunday following receipt of those statements—they are mailed on Monday—always produces our second or third largest offering of the year."

"We do something similar," commented another member of the group, "but it took us about two years to prove to the skeptics it was worth the extra costs in time and postage. We mail twelve statements a year to our people. We're a high turnover congregation, and if we waited to mail that catch-up statement in early December, that would miss a lot of our people who had moved out of town the previous summer. Every month every household in our congregation receives a statement from the financial secretary stating how much they pledged for the year plus their total giving to date. We used to figure we were doing as well as could be expected when we received about 85 percent of what had been pledged. A few contributed more than they pledged, but a lot more only paid half or two-thirds of what they had pledged. Since we began this system, our receipts from pledges are averaging close to 98 or 99 percent."

"That may be a good idea from a practical point of view," objected one man, "but I've never been comfortable with the idea of the church sending statements to people. Our folks already are getting enough bills every month from the gas company, the electric company, department stores, credit card companies, insurance companies, and other places. We used those forms sold by a church supply company for several years. Our financial secretary said they were convenient to use and made the job easier, but we got so many negative comments we decided to drop them."

"So, what are you doing now?" inquired someone else.

The Monthly Letter

"Three years ago we got a new minister who urged us to adopt an improved version of the monthly statement," continued this layperson with increased enthusiasm. "We replaced those statements that looked like bills with monthly form letters. Every month every household in our parish receives a letter, but we have four versions of what is essentially the same letter. The first paragraph describes two or three great things that have happened in ministry or outreach during the past month. The second paragraph points out this would not have been possible without the faithful and regular financial support of our loyal members. The third paragraph lists one or two exciting things just ahead for our church.

"The last paragraph of what is really a form letter comes in four versions. One version expresses tremendous gratitude to those who have contributed at a faster pace than they had pledged. Each of the first three versions includes a sentence with two blank spaces in it. Both blanks are filled out by the financial secretary before she places that letter in an addressed envelope. One blank is the amount pledged and second is the amount contributed through the previous month.

"The second version is for those who have contributed at the pace they had pledged and thanks them for their commitment and for being on schedule. The third version is for those behind on their pledges and points out how it would help if they could catch up on their giving. The fourth version is for those who do not pledge. Most of those are regular or fairly frequent attenders who for one reason or another have chosen not to unite with our church, but many of our nonmembers do pledge."

"Sounds awfully complicated to me," observed the person who had just bragged about sending five statements a year.

"No, it really isn't," came the quick reply. "We have a good office copier so making four versions of the same letter is really very simple. Our financial secretary says the only problem is if the typed envelopes produced by our computer-operated printer are not in the same sequence as her records, she has to do a little shuffling or someone will get the letter with the wrong figures."

"Do you put anything else in that envelope?" asked someone else.

"Yes, since these have to be sent by first-class mail, we include three or four sheets of paper in each one. The first is the form letter I just described. The second is an 8 1/2" x 11" sheet highlighting an upcoming special program or event. The third is a brief and very simple financial statement of the year to date emphasizing what has been accomplished in ministry and a summary of the receipts and expenditures. About a third of the envelopes also contain a personal note or a thank-you from the pastor, the church secretary, or someone chairing a committee. Those personal notes and thank-yous are supposed to be on the financial secretary's desk a day before she does the mailing. She only works one or two days a week, so sometimes we have a little problem with that."

The Array

"The most effective thing we've done to raise our level of giving was started about ten years ago, and it also is done by mail," declared another member of the group. "We had become convinced that while all our people were up-to-date on what it costs to buy a gallon of gasoline, many of them thought it was still 1975 in regard to what a dollar given to

the church will buy. We tried several ways to educate our people to the impact of inflation, but nothing seemed to work until our present minister arrived several years ago. This new pastor sized up the situation quickly and urged that we mail everyone a single sheet of paper. At the top was a brief question, 'Where are you?' Below that was an array with the largest contributions at the top and the smaller ones following in order. We printed the amount given in the previous year by the one hundred largest contributors. There are no names or envelope numbers, only the total contribution last year. Our church also is on a calendar year for the fiscal year, so that was included in the October envelope that also carried the individual statements of giving for the first nine months of the year."

"What was the response?" came a question.

"Just as our new minister had predicted. The new

minister had suggested that in a congregation like ours, there probably would be five or six households, each one of whom thought they should be and were the top contributor. Obviously, not all five or six could be the biggest contributor, but the assumption that they were placed a limit on their giving. A few weeks after this sheet went out and we asked for pledges, five of our largest contributors raised their pledges substantially. All told we got nine pledges for the new year that were in excess of the top figure on that sheet for the previous year. While that sheet was not the only factor, I'm sure it was the most influential single reason behind the 28 percent increase in our pledges."

"Do you still use that same system every year?" inquired someone else.

"We've made only one change since we began," was the reply, "and this also was initiated by our minister. We still publish that list of the top one-hundred contributors of the previous year and none are identified by name or envelope number. The only exception is that opposite one amount is the word 'Pastor.' This lets people know where their minister is in that array. Since our pastor usually ranks about third or fourth in that array, that has had an obviously favorable impact on the giving level of our people."

"Why stop with only a hundred?" asked someone. "Why not list the amount given by every person or family?"

"You may not believe this," came the quick reply, "but we have some families who are long-time members, but they contribute only five or ten dollars a year. We have about two-hundred giving units and we don't want to legitimatize or affirm those who give only a few dollars a year. Our goal is to raise the level of giving, not lower it."

The EMV

"Maybe we're old-fashioned, but the key to the finances in our church is that once a year we call on every member's household and ask everyone to make a financial commitment for the coming year. We have a minister in our regional denominational office who comes out and spends about three hours one evening every year training our people on how to make a call. All of our callers are trained, and we never ask anyone to call for more than two years out of five. We take the pledges received from these calls and that becomes the basis for estimating next year's total receipts. That estimate is the basis for preparing the budget for the coming year." As he described the Every-Member-Visitation program, this sixty-three-year-old congregational leader also made it clear by his voice that he was convinced this was the best approach. "This system has worked for us for at least thirty years, and I hope we'll continue it for another thirty. The only other thing we do is that we have four special offerings for missions on Good Friday, World Communion Sunday, Thanksgiving, and Christmas. That's it. That's our complete financial system."

"We do about the same thing," commented another member of the group, "except we prepare the budget for the coming year and take that proposed budget along to show people when we call on them. We believe when they see the size of the budget and the variety of things we have to spend money on, that will encourage them to be more generous."

MY CONTINUAL COMING ENABLES OTHERS TO BE FORTHCOMING IN FEEDBACK AND FINANCES !

Three calls a year is a great exercise in budget control !
— FRIAR TUCK.

"I would never do that!" declared the first advocate of the Every-Member-Visitation. "That's asking people to give to a budget. That's bad! We want people to make a pledge on the basis of how God has blessed them, not on the basis of helping underwrite a church budget. Our emphasis is on stewardship, not on raising money!"

The Three-Call System

"We also build our system around calling, but our central thrust is not money or the budget or pledges," explained one of the younger members of the group. "Our church has nearly 900 members, and we're convinced that size tends to create alienation, so we try to make three calls every year on every household. The first call, which usually is made in May, is made by a volunteer who has been trained in active listening skills. This call is primarily a get-acquainted and listening call. We want the caller to encourage the persons being called on to express their feelings about their relationship to our church, their hopes, dreams,

wishes, and anything else they want to say including complaints, but we do not solicit gripes. A summary of all these comments, complaints, and dreams is presented to a special meeting of our board in June. These become grist for the mill as we begin to plan program and set goals for the coming year.

"The second call is made about three or four months later, and the callers return to the homes they visited earlier. The first half of that second call is to report on what, if anything, was done in response to what had been heard on that first call," continued this enthusiastic person. "The second half of that second visit is used to present a tentative outline of the proposed program and congregational goals for the coming year, and the caller elicits comments and suggestions on those."

"What does this have to do with expanding the financial base of your congregation?" came an impatient question. "I thought that was the theme of this workshop."

"That is a secondary issue, and I'll get to that in a minute," was the reply. "We're convinced good internal communication is the key to a sound financial base. Our pastor claims that most of the financial crises congregations experience are sparked either by poor internal communication or by a lack of trust by people in the integrity of that church's financial system. The central theme of the three-call system is to improve the quality of the internal communication by listening to the members and making sure they know they've been heard. That second call is to prove to them that they have been heard. The last call has three parts to it. The first is to reestablish the relationship between the visitor and the person being

HMM-M...A STRANGE, LOP-SIDED, END-OF-YEAR ENVELOPE FROM THE CHURCH (?).

Sealed pledges and a statement sent late in the year can make honest folks out of all of us!

—FRIAR TUCK.

called on. That's easy since the same visitor already has been in that home twice in the previous five or six months. The second part is to present the proposed program and budget for the coming year and to answer questions about both the program and the budget. The third part is to ask for a pledge for the coming year."

Grace Giving

"We come from a different background than many of you," observed one of the quieter participants in that workshop, "and we don't ask for pledges the way some of you do. Our basic assumption is that it is only through the grace of God that we live to see another day and that all our material possessions are given to us by the grace of God. When it comes to how we deal with financing the life and ministry of our church, this assumption influences what we do and how we do it.

First, we believe the financial commitment of a member is between that individual and God, not between the member and the congregation. When financial pledges are made, each person or family signs a pledge card indicating the amount of money they intend to contribute to that congregation during the coming year. That pledge card is placed in an envelope with the member's name on the outside. The envelope is sealed and turned in with the other pledges, perhaps in a special ceremony on a particular Sunday. It is never opened! At the end of the year, the unopened envelope is returned to the member with a statement of how much money that member gave during the year."

"How can your finance committee prepare a budget for the coming year if they don't know how much people have pledged?" interrupted the sixty-three-year-old advocate of the Every-Member Canvass.

"By faith," came the reply. "Our finance committee prepares a budget on the basis of needs rather than on anticipated income. After all, if we live by the grace of God, and if it is God who gives us another day, is it not reasonable to assume that God will provide for our needs, both individually and corporately? Third, since our congregation lives by the grace of God, it is not necessary to lay aside reserves for the future. The congregation promises to spend or give away all the money received during the year. Insofar as it is administratively possible, our church always tries to end the year with a zero balance in the treasury. Sometimes that requires a special meeting to decide where the surplus will go, but we usually succeed in ending the year with an empty treasury."

"We do, too, but we also usually have a bunch of leftover bills that haven't been paid," commented someone with a sour smile.

Faith Promise

"The system we use is something like Grace Giving," reflected an elderly participant, "but we call it Faith Promise. Everyone is asked to make a financial commitment for the coming year on the assumption that if God gives you another year, He will provide all you need to live a faithful life. The promise half is if your income exceeds your expectations, you

Sometimes...
I'm overwhelmed by
the goodness of others!
—FRIAR TUCK

promise to return to the Lord, via the church, a tithe of that additional income."

Monthly Mailing of Envelopes

"You folks overwhelm me with what apparently is a high level of commitment by your members and an equally high energy level," reflected another participant. "I've been sitting here thinking that if I went home and proposed that we call on every member three times in seven months, our church council would adopt a rule prohibiting any member ever again to attend any workshop. While it doesn't produce the level of giving we really should have in our church, we adopted a fairly simple system two years ago that both broadened the number of regular contributors and also raised our total giving by nearly 15 percent."

"Quick, tell us what it is," came an eager response. "That's what our church needs. A simple system that

will raise our level of giving, but not be too much work."

"Well, it is some extra work," came the reply, "but it has worked for us. Every month on the Monday following the last Sunday of that month, we gather together a group of about a dozen mature adult volunteers and we mail everyone a set of four or five envelopes for the next month. Each envelope we mail includes the offering envelopes for that next month plus a form letter telling people about the state of finances. That's the only change we've made in our financial system in the past dozen years, and that one change has taken us from an era when we had perpetual cash flow problems to the point that now August is the only month when we have a problem, and I guess August is a problem for everyone."

Envelopes Do Work!

"Yes, envelopes do work," affirmed one of the seven pastors attending that workshop. "I come from a denominational tradition that has been extremely reluctant to adopt anything that resembled a business technique. Most of our churches are rural and while our support for missions always has been good, our overall level of giving is nothing to brag about. In each of my four pastorates I have introduced the idea of providing a box of offering envelopes for every member, including the children. I'm convinced that is the simplest, easiest, and most effective way to teach stewardship, increase the frequency of worship attendance and raise the level of giving. If your congregation is not now using offering envelopes, I'm convinced that is the first change you should recommend when you go home from this workshop. Up until a couple of minutes ago, I had never heard of mailing them out monthly, but we may try that."

Change the Fiscal Year

"How many of you come from a congregation that uses the calendar year for your fiscal year?" asked a person who had been waiting impatiently for a chance to speak. About two-thirds of the hands went up in response to that question.

"We did, too, ever since our church was organized in 1957," continued this advocate of a different approach, "but we suddenly realized one day the Tax Reform Act of 1986 made that an obsolete concept. The new tax law reduces the number of items that people can deduct from their income when calculating their income tax. The net result is more and more people are bunching their deductions into alternate calendar years and taking the standard deduction the following year. So we've changed our fiscal year to accommodate that. We now use a July 1 to June 30 fiscal year. That means members can, for example, delay their contributions for the 1989–90 church year to the first half of 1990 and make their contributions for the 1990–91 church year during the last six months of 1990. That enables them to bunch two years of charitable contributions into one tax year, and they can take the standard deductions in 1989

A fiscal year that runs from July to June enables us to be generous at a time when we can best afford it!

and 1991. Rather than postpone their giving for one full year, which our church cannot afford to encourage, or to expect them to make a full year's contributions a year in advance, which most of our people can't do, changing our fiscal year means they postpone one year's contributions for only six months and they have to make advance contributions for only six months."

"That sounds terribly complicated, and I cannot understand the benefits," objected a perplexed individual.

"The summer-to-summer fiscal year has several other advantages," added someone who clearly saw this to be a useful concept. "For many churches the program year coincides with the school year. This makes the fiscal year fit the program year. In addition, by making the term of office for leaders fit the fiscal and program year, that means we nominate people in the spring, elect them at the annual meeting held about two weeks before the public schools let out. That's more convenient than trying to nominate people at the beginning of the busy Christmas season. Also where I live in Montana, we do better getting people to come to an annual meeting held in mid-May rather than one held in January. The newly elected officers take office before the beginning of the new program year in August, rather than in January in the middle of the program year. This also means we ask our people to make financial pledges late in April or early May, which everyone knows is a better time than November to ask people to make financial commitments."

"What makes you think spring is better than November for asking people to make pledges?" questioned the person who had expressed perplexity over the basic concept.

"First, because the

Spring Giving

After taxes is a great time to do spring-cleaning of our wallets and purses!

—FRIAR TUCK

surveys conducted by the big fund-raising companies list November as a bad month and identify April and May as positive months," replied this advocate of a summer-to-summer fiscal year. "Second, the general climate of opinion is more optimistic in the spring than in November. The days are getting longer, the flowers are blooming, the grass is greener, the milk is richer, the birds are singing, people are looking forward to summer, and the death rate is declining. Third, that is when millions of people are looking forward to receiving their income tax refund. In November they are looking ahead to a pile of Christmas bills and, where I live, much higher costs for heating their homes. Fourth, when people have just completed making out their income tax returns, they have a more realistic understanding of their income than they had the previous November. Fifth, the financial campaign can be related to the new program year rather than to a program year well under way. The future always looks more exciting than the present. Sixth, the best time for a big financial campaign is as close as possible following the big annual celebration of the resurrection of our Lord and Savior. Finally, as was just pointed out, national tax policy now encourages more than ever the concept that for many people it is fiscally wise to bunch all charitable contributions in alternate years and take the standard deduction in other years. Asking for pledges in April or May for a fiscal year beginning the first of June or the first of July facilitates this."

"I don't think I could explain all of that to our people back home," reflected the person who earlier had described this as highly complicated.

"We're simply trying to offer a range of possibilities," comforted the leader of the workshop. "Be selective. Pick and choose what you think is appropriate for your situation back home and forget the rest."

"I must confess I am not sure changing the fiscal year will solve all our problems, and it may add a new one by upsetting the folks at denominational headquarters who insist we do our reporting on a calendar year," added one of the pastors in the group.

"That shouldn't be a problem," interrupted the man from Montana who obviously had more to say on his pet theme. "I expect you provide monthly financial statements for your governing board. You can take twelve consecutive monthly reports for January through December to prepare your parish report to denominational headquarters and use a July through June set of monthly reports to prepare the report to your members.

"While I've got the floor," he continued, "let me point out two more advantages of the July to June fiscal year. A lot of people catch up on their giving near the end of the calendar year for tax reasons. A couple of you have pointed that out already. Others catch up just before the end of the church's fiscal year. If the fiscal year is the calendar year, that is December. When the fiscal year ends in June, you have two catch-up periods. One in December for tax purposes and one in June at the end of the church year. That gives you two times to send out powerful reminders. In addition, as people catch up on their giving before the end of

Caution: Separation of church and state is often seen as the state separating the church from its offerings!

the church year in June, that produces extra income to help carry through what otherwise would be the cash flow squeeze months. Our people in our denominational headquarters have never complained when we send our biggest check of the year in the first week of July. The other advantage is that well over two-thirds of the families who move in any one year do so between mid-May and mid-September. You can take prospective moves into account more easily when you are nominating officers or asking for pledges in April or May than if you do that in November."

The 5 Percent Club

"What I started to say," continued the pastor who was glad to regain the floor, "is that I've used a fairly simple system in three different churches that has enabled us to launch new programs or meet needs that

Oh...Oh... It looks like
the Pastor's
Five Percent Club
is on the move again!

were not covered by the budget. In each case I waited until my second year when I went out and recruited twenty people to be members of what I called the '5 Percent Club.' I invited these members to our home and explained that needs outside the budget would arise. I told them I needed twenty people, each of whom would give as second-mile contributions 5 percent of the cost of such needs. I promised them they could decide whether what I presented was a legitimate need. I also told them we would meet no more than twice a year. If I brought in an idea to one of these meetings and they voted it down, that used up half of the quota for that year. I also promised that I would not bring in anything that cost more than $5,000. That meant their maximum liability would be $250 once or twice a year. Twenty gifts of $250 each equals $5,000. In the first church where I tried this, I had to ask thirty-three people to get my twenty. In my present parish I asked only twenty-four and I got twenty positive responses. It now looks as if there is enough interest to create a second '5 Percent Club' next year in the church I'm now serving."

"Sounds like an elite group," said another minister. "I'm not sure I would be comfortable with that."

"Yup, it is an elite group," declared the proponent of the plan. "The twelve apostles were picked to be an elite group. When I was ordained a Christian minister, I joined an elite group. We try to convince our Sunday school teachers and every one of our board members as well as all three of our choirs that each is in an elite group. If you're not comfortable with the idea of an elite group, don't do it!"

Priming the pump can increase the flow of God's grace in any church!

—FRIAR TUCK

Three-Budget System

"I can affirm the concept that Christians should see themselves as an elite and set-apart group," affirmed a layperson, "but my impression is our society is moving away from highly disciplined, elite groups, which accept the high expectations placed on them by becoming followers of the Christ. Our church back home really acts more like a voluntary society. Some of our members express a much higher level of commitment than do others. We have some members who never miss church on Sunday morning unless they're out-of-town or sick. Others come once or twice a month. A fair number show up only a few Sundays a year. That's the context for what we do. Our previous minister preached frequently on the need for a higher level of commitment by all members, but his exhortations didn't have much effect. When he left, our new minister agreed we had to do something because we were clearly underfinanced. So, to make a long story short, we now prepare three budgets. One is for the

Three-Budget System

"O Creator, Redeemer
and Sustainer,
we ask your blessings
for the mortgage,
maintenance
and missions..."

—FRIAR TUCK

regular operating expenses such as salaries, utilities, supplies, and insurance; a second is for payments on a mortgage that still has seven years left on it; and the third is for missions. The operating budget is financed by the weekly offerings and regular pledges while the other two budgets are supported by designated contributions and special appeals. The year before we first began this system our total receipts from member giving came to a total of $138,500. The first year of the three-budget system member giving jumped to $161,000—that's an increase of almost $23,000 in one year! About half of that increase was money designated for missions. Our mortgage payments run about $1,800 a month and now that is all underwritten outside the budget. We discovered a lot of people like to designate where their money will go. The biggest increases in giving came from among our less active members, which I guess is no surprise to anyone."

God's Acre

"I guess I may be the only person here from a farming community church," observed a seventy-year-old man as he looked at the hands of the others in the room. "My wife and I have been members of the same little open country church for all of our lives. Back during the Depression of the 1930s we got a preacher who introduced us to the Lord's acre concept. Every year every farm sets aside one acre of land. Whatever that acre yields is sold and the money goes to the church. I grew up on an eighty-acre farm and that meant a little over 1 percent of our farm was set aside to produce for God. Now my two boys and I run a total of nearly

It can cause the smallest of churches to produce a divine harvest!

—FRIAR TUCK

1,600 acres, so we set aside what we grow on sixteen acres for the church. In a good year those sixteen acres will clear somewhere between $1,500 and $3,000 depending on prices and on the weather. We still have eight farmers left in the congregation who do this. When you add what we get from the Lord's acre to our regular giving, that's the difference between our little church being able to stay open or being forced to close."

"What's your worship attendance on Sunday morning?" inquired one of the pastors in the group.

"It averages between thirty and thirty-five, about the same as it was forty years ago," replied the farmer.

"What's your budget?" asked another minister.

"Well, we don't have an elaborate budget," explained the farmer. "We really don't see the need for that. We have a forty-seven-year-old minister who was widowed when she was thirty-eight. About four years after her husband's death, she felt a call to preach and

Too much
of a good thing
can limit our zip,
lessen our zing!

—FRIAR TUCK

went to seminary. The minister we had for nearly thirty years was ready to retire, so she came directly from seminary five years ago to follow him. We provide her with a house, utilities, insurance, and travel, and pay a cash salary of $22,000.

"Wow!" exclaimed one of the ministers, "that's more than I get, and I serve a congregation four times as large."

"Well, you're younger and you don't have the experience our minister has," explained the farmer. "In addition to being widowed, she has a twenty-two-year-old handicapped daughter who lives with her. She knows what life is all about."

"What were your total expenditures last year and how much did you give for missions?" inquired another minister who clearly was intrigued by what obviously was an unusual situation.

Well, I'm not sure exactly what last year came to," replied the farmer, "but my guess is we took in a total of about $55,000, and a third of that went for missions. Years ago we adopted a rule that thirty-three cents out of every dollar we receive goes to missions."

"I guess that explains why your minister has a higher salary than mine," reflected the minister who a moment earlier had exclaimed over that $22,000 cash salary. "We average 125 at worship and last year our total member-giving came to less than twice that."

"The Lord's acre makes a difference," explained the farmer very simply.

Post the Bills

"We don't have any farmers in our church back home," commented another member of the group, "and maybe that's our problem. We also have had five different ministers in eight years, but that's another story. The closest I can come to sharing

May your church reap the rewards of such redemptive rip-offs!

a success story grows out of the fact that every vacancy period between ministers sees the attendance drop off and of course that means the offerings also go down. Twice now in the past three years our treasurer has come in to the monthly board meeting with over $3,500 in unpaid bills outstanding. The first time it happened, someone suggested we simply post a bunch of pieces of paper on a bulletin board, with each piece of paper representing one bill. One piece of paper had written on it $81.70 for office supplies, another was the electric bill, and a third was the insurance bill. The biggest was a couple of hundred dollars, and the smallest was a little under ten dollars. That Sunday we asked those present to pick a bill off the bulletin board and give it and the money necessary to pay it to the treasurer. Ten days later all the bills were paid. A couple of months ago we had another bunch of unpaid bills and we did the same thing, except this time we sent

Going once,
twice, three times
on behalf of
our Highest Giver!

a letter to every member listing the bills and the amount of each one. The following Tuesday they were all paid."

"We did something similar," recalled someone, "except instead of posting them on the bulletin board, our moderator held the actual bills and called off the amount at our annual meeting in January. The moderator asked for volunteers and before we adjourned, all those unpaid bills had been taken care of and we could report we no longer had a deficit."

The Auction

"I can remember the Lord's acre from when I grew up on a farm," explained an older man, "but the church we're now in has only a couple of farmers. The economic base for our community has changed during the past dozen years from agricultural to tourists and retirees. So we have a big auction every August at the peak of the tourist season. Our people donate everything from fancy quilts to garden produce, from antiques to toys. One of our members is a new car dealer and he always contributes a good used car. Another member is an auctioneer and every year on the second Saturday in August we auction off all these donations. About a month earlier we nail auction posters to telephone posts and place them in store windows all around the community and also put a notice in the local weekly paper. On the day of the auction we serve refreshments, including homemade pies, cakes, and ice cream, hot dogs, hamburgers, and other food. Last year we cleared nearly $18,000 all told. One-half of everything we make goes to missions and one-half goes into the budget. The tourists really flock to the auctions!"

"We're also located in an area that attracts a lot of tourists," commented a mature woman, "so we've moved our bazaar from mid–November to early August and from the basement of the church to a big tent we rent and set up in the yard. The tent is open on all sides. We also now have an auctioneer. The stuff we used to sell for a couple of dollars at the bazaar not brings five to ten dollars at the auction. We've more than tripled the proceeds from the bazaar by moving it outside and using an auctioneer. You're right, Jim, an auction draws those tourists in a way the bazaar in the church basement never did."

"I hate to sound like a wet blanket," protested the youngest woman in the group, "but this workshop was supposed to be about expanding your church's financial base, and now we're talking about getting the money to pay the bills from tourists and auctions. I'm convinced the members ought to pay all the costs of running the church, and, if they won't do that, maybe that church should close! I want to focus on how to raise the level of stewardship among the members."

"That's what the morning was all about," reminded the man from Montana. "The schedule called for a sharing of back-home experiences after lunch, and that's what we've been doing."

Assumptions, Values, and Goals

That difference in perspective may offer a good time to change the subject briefly and to review the point of this

Item: The cost of human, person-centered services, has risen much faster than our incomes!

—FRIAR TUCK

narrative. The first part of this chapter represents an attempt to review a variety of methods and approaches congregations use to broaden the financial base for ministry and outreach.

In evaluating these alternatives, four points should be kept in mind. First, as should be apparent from the sequence of the chapters, the value system of both authors places stewardship and stewardship education at the top of the priority list. That is the best single approach. It must be recognized, however, that in tens of thousands of Christian congregations, both Protestant and Catholic, the level of member giving is not sufficient to underwrite the financial costs of ministry.

A broad, simple (and excessively simplistic) general explanation of that fact of life is that the costs of providing person-centered services have gone up far more rapidly since 1950 than people's incomes have risen. This can be illustrated by looking at the costs for operating hospitals, public schools, the judicial system, nursing homes, churches, theological seminaries, colleges, universities, and prisons, or for a visit to a physician. The big increases in productivity have come in the production of food, fibre, retail trade, and the manufacturing of products, not in person-centered services. The costs of producing a bushel of wheat have gone down dramatically while the costs of maintaining a three-hundred-member congregation have gone up.

NOT JUST PIE·IN·THE·SKY WHEN WE DIE BUT SOMETHING ON OUR PLATE WHILE WE WAIT!

Whatever we feel good about giving is what God wants from us!

—FRIAR TUCK

Second, stewardship education, like house-work or cleaning off my desk, is a job that is never completed. Most congregations resemble a passing parade, not a static collection of people. A fairly common pattern is that the turn-over rate among one-half of the membership is approximately 3 percent annually while 10 to 15 percent of the other half leave every year. A continuing program of stewardship education can be the central component of a long-term financial strategy, but often it must be supplemented by short-term tactics such as described in this chapter.

Third, and perhaps most significant, should the financial system of your congregation be based solely on people contributing money? Should it be based on the assumption that a cash economy is part of the biblical mandate? Or should it be based on the assumption that people can and should be encouraged to contribute to the propagation of the gospel out of their income, energy, time, accumulated wealth, creativity, skills, experience, and talent? This chapter is based on an affirmative response to this last assumption. For many people baking a pie or helping erect a tent or making something to be contributed to the auction or singing in the choir or acting in a play or raising some corn to be sold with the proceeds going to the church or making a quilt that sells for $400 may be a more meaningful contribution to the Lord's work than writing a check for $200.

In addition, in a great many congregations participation in these activities may be one of the few open doors for prospective new members to gain a sense of belonging in what often is a largely closed fellowship.

Finally, and for many readers the central question can be stated simply. Which of the suggestions contained in this chapter are consistent with the values you affirm and the goals you can support? As one of the participants in this workshop, and an articulate supporter of the annual auction in his church, explained, "One of our goals is to increase the level of giving by that one-half of our members who give less than 1 percent of their annual income to our church. That's one of our long-term goals. Among my short-term goals are these three: (1) to make sure all our creditors are paid within thirty days after they submit their bills, (2) to expand our total program, and (3) to allocate at least one-fourth of our total receipts to missions. The auction helped us meet all three of those short-term goals."

Revise the Organizational Structure

Now, to return to the central theme of this chapter, it may be appropriate to look at what may be the most complicated suggestion for expanding the financial base of your congregation. This is to revise the organizational structure. The majority of Protestant congregations are not organized to teach stewardship or to encourage a higher level of giving. They are organized to minimize expenditures. This can be illustrated by asking one question.

What is the *primary* responsibility of the finance committee in your congregation?

Is the *primary* responsibility to prepare a budget for the next year? Or to make sure the contributions of the members are sufficient to cover all necessary expenditures? Or to oversee the financial scene so expenditures do not exceed receipts? Or to determine the order of priorities in ministry for the next year? Or to model and teach Christian stewardship? Or to encourage all members to tithe? Or to oversee this congrega-

Stewardship

With a world in need, the least of our concerns should be keeping our expenditures to a minimum!

— FRIAR TUCK

tion's investment portfolio? Or to conduct an annual financial campaign? Or to encourage members to remember this church in their will? Or to look ahead and plan for the financial undergirding of the ministry of this congregation three years down the road? Or to reduce to a reasonable figure the requests from various committees and departments for funds for next year? Or to concentrate on how to expand the financial base of this congregation and encourage a broader base of financial support from among the members?

If your answer is, "all of the above," you missed the key word in the question! It is somewhere between unreasonable and irresponsible to expect any one committee to carry more than one (or possibly two) *primary* responsibilities. This observer's experiences suggest the vast majority of Protestant congregations on this continent project unrealistic and contradictory expectations of their finance committee.

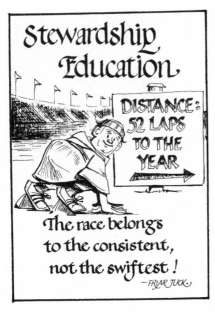

Stewardship Education

DISTANCE: 52 LAPS TO THE YEAR

The race belongs to the consistent, not the swiftest!

—FRIAR TUCK

The most common expectation is that this one committee will (a) model and teach stewardship, (b) prepare a budget that will undergird an expansion of the ministry of that congregation, (c) reduce proposed expenditures to match anticipated receipts, and (d) make sure the budget is fully funded. When contradictory or incompatible expectations are placed on an individual, or on a committee, the predictable responses usually include (a) a feeling of frustration, (b) a positive response to one expectation, and (c) an effort to rationalize disobeying or ignoring or neglecting other expectations that are not consistent with the course of action that has been chosen.

When these conflicting expectations are placed on the finance committee, it should not be surprising to discover that a powerful motivating factor in that committee's deliberations will be to minimize expenditures. The conflicts in role that often are created by placing excessive and contradictory expectations on the finance committee can by illustrated by two examples.

The first example comes with the beginning of the new fiscal year when many finance committees have the responsibility for (a) setting priorities in expenditures, (b) preparing the final budget for the coming year, and (c) conducting the every-member-visitation program or whatever system will be used to secure commitments of anticipated contributions from the members.

Raising money is much more fun than cutting back expenses!
—FRIAR TUCK

In preparing the budget for the coming year the finance committee acts as a priority-setting group in deciding what should be the highest priorities in undergirding, reinforcing, and expanding the ministry and outreach of that congregation. Naturally, that will make them function as advocates of an expanded budget. At the same time they also are responsible for making sure anticipated expenditures will not exceed the projected income. That makes the finance committee an advocate for a thrifty set of expenditures. Which role should dominate the thinking of the members of the finance committee? Expanding ministry or minimizing expenditures? If the *primary* basis for the evaluation of their work is the numerical growth of the congregation, they may place a higher priority on a sharp increase in expenditures in order to fund new ministries. If, however, the primary basis for evaluating their work is that expenditures do not exceed receipts, they may be more concerned with minimizing expenditures. The basic generalization in our society is that anyone charged with the responsibility for paying the bills naturally will favor minimizing expenditures.

A second example often comes up at the September meeting of the governing board when the treasurer

Is your Finance Committee tied in knots because it has too many strings to pull?

—FRIAR TUCK

reports that contributions for the first eight months came to only 59 percent of the anticipated goal for the year, but expenditures have been 71 percent of the amount budgeted for the year. What will be the response of the finance committee to that report? Will it favor a special fund-raising program to make up the difference? Or will it favor cutting back on expenditures for the rest of the year? The members of the finance committee probably will choose the alternative which (a) matches their greatest competence, (b) appears to be the easier course of action, and (c) fits the role in which they feel most comfortable and have the most practice.

One alternative is to continue to place excessive expectations on the finance committee and recognize that the limitations of financial resources will be a powerful force in determining priorities. Another alternative is to divide these responsibilities among three different committees. This, or course, will be more appealing to congregations including two hundred or more members, since size may limit the number of volunteers available for a more complex structure.

Perhaps the easiest of these three committees to describe, since it already exists in many congregations, is the committee on stewardship. Typically this committee has three overlapping responsibilities: (1) providing stewardship education, (2) enlisting a cadre of tithers, and (3) encouraging people to include this church in their will. Normally it has neither the authority nor responsibility for the allocation of current income.

A second committee has the basic responsibility for preparing a comprehensive budget for the coming year. Sometimes this is done as part of a three- or four- or five-year financial plan for that congregation. Ideally, the three criteria that dominate the decision-making processes of this committee will be (1) obedience to what the members believe the Lord is calling this congregation to be and to do, (2) matching the priorities in the allocation of funds with the mission statement or the priorities in ministry of that congregation, and (3) making sure the funds allocated to "housekeeping" and care of the members are not excessive when compared to the funds designated for outreach and mission. No higher than fourth on that list of criteria will be the goal of keeping expenditures to a minimum.

In this organizational structure a third group, the finance committee, normally has one—and only one— primary responsibility. That is to make sure the money received is at least equal to the anticipated expenditures. Perhaps the clearest way of stating that is to state the opposite. The finance committee does *not* have the responsibility to make sure the budget does not exceed anticipated receipts! The budget committee has the sole authority over expenditures—subject in most congregations to the oversight of the governing board. In this system the budget preparation committee is concerned only with the expenditures side of the ledger. Ministry and outreach, not minimizing expenditures, is the dominant force for the budget committee while the finance committee worries about the income side.

As many readers already have guessed, the experience with this system produces at least a fifty-fifty probability that the budget committee will approve

expenditures in excess of what the finance committee views as realistic in terms of anticipated income. This can be expected to produce two or three or four financial crises in the typical year as contributions fall behind expenditures.

At this point the system tends to enable the call to ministry to overcome prudence. First, in what some identify as a series of minor miracles, the money is forthcoming. Instead of responding to normal institutional pressures to cut back on expenditures, this system usually places a higher priority on raising more money, frequently by special appeals, such as those described in chapters 3 and 4 or by some of the alternatives described earlier in this chapter.

Second, and far more significant, contrary to all concepts of prudent fiscal management, the most vital congregations tend to resolve one fiscal crisis only to be confronted by a new one a few months later. By contrast, those congregations in which the month's receipts nearly always exceed the expenditures frequently display many signs of passivity, complacency, and a strong orientation to the status quo or to the past.

Among the reasons for what appears to be a paradox is that the congregations that prepare the budget based on obedience to the Lord, a call to ministry, and a desire to expand the outreach of that church, rather than on the basis of cautiously projected income, also tend to be venturesome risk-taking, future-oriented, and confident congregations convinced that if the Lord calls, the Lord also will provide. In simple terms these congregations display a deeply rooted hope in tomorrow and are not restricted by yesterday's financial experiences or traditions. (*Caution:* Extravagant financial projections usually will not by

That Fourth Committee

YEAR-AROUND AUDITING

It audits our integrity, intentionality and industry!
— FRIAR TUCK

themselves create this venturesome, hope-filled, future-oriented, and confident spirit within a congregation! The optimistic financial projections are a product, not a cause of this type of congregational attitudes.)

In considering this organizational structure it would be unwise to neglect the power of (1) the sinful nature of human beings, (2) institutional pressures, (3) tradition, and (4) the feelings of those who are convinced the churches should minimize expenditures of money.

Therefore it may be wise to look at a fourth group for this system of independent and non-overlapping committees. This is the audit committee that functions in a watchdog capacity similar to the General Accounting Office of the United States government. This committee might have a many as six mutually compatible responsibilities: (1) the annual financial audit to ensure the integrity of the financial administration of that congregation, (2) an annual audit to

determine the compatibility between the actual expenditures and mission statement or the programmatic goals, (3) an occasional audit of a particular program to determine whether that program is compatible with and supportive of congregation-wide goals, and (4) an occasional audit of the expenditure of the time of each paid staff member to determine whether the actual expenditure of time is consistent with the expectations placed on the person holding that position. Each audit report could be accompanied by suggestions for improvement and/or recommendations in regard to specific goals and policies. In addition, this committee might review (5) the stewardship of time and energy of the governing board and/or (6) the stewardship in the utilization of the real estate.

Dozens of congregations have attempted to implement of variation of this basic system by creating two or three subcommittees within the finance committee. Too often the result is (1) one or more responsibilities (usually stewardship education and the audits) continue to be neglected, and/or (2) the dominant institutional pressures continue to be the goal of keeping expenditures within receipts rather than expanding the financial base, and/or (3) prudence overwhelms venturesomeness and hope. The creation of separate and independent committees may be the most effective means of reducing the excessive, and often incompatible expectations, placed on one committee as well as a means for expanding the financial base.

Leaders from a majority of congregations will respond, "We simply have too few members to staff such an elaborate committee structure. We have to limit ourselves to one committee that is responsible for all aspects of stewardship and finance." If that is

— FRIAR TUCK

Gimmicks can quicken heart, hand and purse coordination

true, and that may not be an accurate appraisal, two points emerge. The first is, do not be surprised if a dominant theme in the deliberations of that committee turns out to be to minimize expenditures. If that does occur, the next question may be, What are some other sources for supplementing our financial base? That takes us back to the central theme of this chapter.

Buy a Brick

One Sunday morning as the members began to arrive for Sunday school at a Colorado church, they found the double doors leading from the narthex into the sanctuary and the entrance from the parking lot hidden behind a wall of cardboard bricks. Two dozen teenagers were prepared for the early arrivals and announced, "You folks have been talking about renovating the fellowship hall for more that three years. We've decided the time has come for a decision and the best way to make a decision is to start a building fund. These bricks are $10 apiece and we have 5,000 of them for sale. You may buy as many as you want. When they're all sold, the doors will be opened. Approximately 45 minutes later (a) the bricks had all been sold, many with an IOU, (b) $50,000 had been collected for the building fund, (c) Sunday school had been cancelled for the day, and (d) the adults had concluded the time had come to begin to plan for the renovation of the fellowship hall.

In another congregation the bricks from the demolition of the old Sunday school wing were sold at a dollar each to raise money for the furnishings of the new educational building. Dozens of congregations have "sold" parking spaces to pay for the acquisition or paving or resurfacing of that church's parking lot. A parallel plan is to sell the granite blocks that mark the path in the memory lane walk across the lawn or through the parish's garden.

This is clearly a "gimmick," but it also is a means of arousing interest as well as securing additional funds.

Bet on Inflation

"We sure were lucky we decided to build when we did," reflected a long-time member at the Woodbury Church. "At the time, back in 1969, we had a lot of opposition when we decided to spend $240,000 for the construction of a new sanctuary. It would cost at least a million dollars today to duplicate what we have here. In addition, we financed most of the cost with a twenty-year mortgage. That meant for the past several years we have been using thirty-cent dollars to pay off those dollars we borrowed back in 1968."

A highly productive, if indirect, source of money for paying off mortgages taken out in the late 1960s, the

1970s, and the early 1980s was inflation. Many congregations found themselves in a situation parallel to that of the Woodbury Church. The new building cost them $240,000 in 1969. The interest on a twenty-year mortgage came to $375,000. That meant that in 1989 they had constructed a building that would cost over $1,000,000 to reproduce at a cost of $615,000 including interest payments. That arrange-

You can bet on inflation!

— FRIAR TUCK

ment also meant the new building was paid for by those who used it, not just those who dreamed up the idea back in 1968.

If another big round of inflation in the 1990s turns out to be the means used to reduce the impact of the interest payments on the national budget, it might be wise for churches to finance major capital improvement programs with a large long-term mortgage. Inflation was the means used to offset the impact of a rising national debt between 1944 and 1981. Will that happen again in the future?

If the answer turns out to be affirmative, that could be a wonderful source for churches to use in financing building programs. If, however, history does not repeat itself, that could be a disaster paralleling what happened in many congregations that went into debt for new buildings in the 1925–31 era. What do you expect will happen?

The Trustees' Fund

In most congregations the easiest money to raise is for new buildings. The second easiest is for the care and renovation of existing structures. The hardest money to raise often is that required to expand the staff in order to broaden the program.

Do those three generalizations fit your congregation? If they do, you may want to consider creation of a separate trustees' fund. While many variations can be found for this approach, the typical trustees' fund exists for several reasons, including (1) to provide the trustees with a predictable and dependable source of funds for the maintenance of what often is an old structure, (2) to encourage people to contribute to that fund directly through designated gifts, memorials, and bequests, (3) to take advantage of the appeal of this sacred meeting place, (4) to keep those relatively easy-to-meet financial demands out of the regular budget so those funds can be allocated for ministry and outreach, (5) to compensate for the fact that in many congregations it is difficult to anticipate all the needs of the trustees and that their needs may vary substantially from year to year, and (6) to take advantage of the fact that preventive maintenance often is less expensive than repairs.

While the separate trustees fund can be a supplemental source of income, it frequently evokes considerable opposition from those who prefer a unified budget.

The Role of Organizations

One of the significant differences between Anglo congregations and black churches is that black churches often place a far greater emphasis on the value of organizations (usher board, choir, deacons, Sunday school, women's organizations, credit union) than do Anglo congregations.

Among the predominantly Anglo denominations big differences exist in terms of the importance of organizations. For example, congregations affiliated with the Southern Baptist Convention usually place a far greater emphasis on the importance of organizations than do churches affiliated with the Evangelical Lutheran Church in America or the United Church of Christ.

... AND IN THIS GAME, EACH OF YOU GETS TO CARRY YOUR OWN BALL!

CHURCH SCHOOL

MEN'S FELLOWSHIP

CHOIR

May thy treasury be blessed with abundant treasurers!

—FRIAR TUCK

In some congregations the organizations represent a prolific supplemental source of funds. These may range from the money contributed to the regular budget by an adult Sunday school class to the funds for renovation of the kitchen contributed by another organization to the scholarships from the men's fellowship for children going to summer camp. It is not at all uncommon in some traditions to find that one-half to three-quarters of all money given for missions in any one year comes from various organizations rather than from the general treasury. In scores of congregations the Sunday school is a more prolific source of funds than the Sunday morning worship service.

Organizations can be even more valuable as entry points for the reception and assimilation of new members. A widely used method for undermining the life, vitality, outreach, and influence of the organizational life of a congregation is to adopt a rule abolishing all separate treasuries and eliminating all positions called treasurer except for the one person who is the treasurer for the entire congregation. The healthiest organizations with the longest life expectancy have learned to ignore both such rules and those who urge adoption of them.

The Power of the Visual

For many people today television, not the printed word, is the primary channel for the communication of current news. When this concept is carried into the church, it can have amazing results.

"Please be seated, I have some interesting news for you," offered the attorney as he greeted the senior minister from First Church. "I asked you to come over this morning so I could explain to you the terms of Walter Brown's will. To put it very simply, you have your chapel."

"I haven't the faintest idea of what you're talking about," replied the pastor.

"About five years ago Walter, who has been one of my clients ever since I set up my practice forty-three years ago," continued the attorney, "came over and said he wanted to include in his will enough money to cover the cost of that new chapel you wanted. As nearly as I could understand the story, your parish hired an architect several years ago who prepared some renderings of various improvements you folks wanted to make at First Church. Apparently these colored pictures were hung on the wall in one of the corridors and Walter was taken with the proposal for a chapel. He came to me to revise his will. I had no idea how much money was involved and Walter didn't either, so I called the architect. He gave us an estimate of $300,000. Walter decided that wasn't enough; he figured building costs would be much higher by the time he died, so he told me to include the $600,000 for the chapel in his will."

"Walter never had that kind of money!" interrupted the pastor. "I knew him very well, and his whole estate won't come to $600,000, and I know there are other heirs."

"You're a little low," corrected the attorney. "Walter's entire estate comes to well over $2,000,000. His closest heirs are two nephews and he left them each a half million. He divided the rest among several charitable causes, and your parish is in it for $600,000 for a chapel."

"I'm absolutely overwhelmed," declared the pastor. "I can't remember ever saying one word to Walter about that proposal for a chapel."

"Apparently it wasn't necessary," replied the attorney. "The picture on the wall told Walter all he wanted to know."

Far more common is the practice of many churches to post on the wall in a corridor a picture of a current need. In one congregation a large panel on the wall carries the words,

THIS MONTH'S TOP PRIORITY.

Underneath those words a new picture is posted each month. One month it is a picture of a starving child as a part of that month's emphasis on relief of worldwide hunger. Another month it is a picture of a church-related black college that congregation helps support. Another month it was the color photograph of the new

A picture...

...can be worth
a thousand dollars!

—*FRIAR TUCK*

van needed to replace the church's worn-out vehicle. One time the display consisted of one copy of the hymnal recently adopted by that denomination. Once a year it is a recent picture of the missionary family that congregation helps support. Below the panel is a box with a slot in the top for people to drop checks and money into if they choose to support that special need.

Many more churches use slides or videotapes to explain the budget for the coming year or to lift up some other special need. All these are examples of the power of visual communication in communicating needs to people who have the resources necessary to meet those needs. (*Caution!* Whenever people are encouraged to contribute to a designated cause, it is absolutely essential that all the funds go to that cause! One of the most effective means of undercutting people's confidence in the financial system of your congregation is to divert the money given to a specific cause to some other use.)

The Workshop

"Our Hunger Commission sponsors a workshop every October," explained a woman from Central Church. "The themes vary from year to year. Our committee picks the topic, brings in a resource person, publicizes it, handles all the advance registrations, prepares and serves the meals and refreshments, rents the table, sets up the room, registers the people when they come, and cleans up afterward. It is a lot of work, but we achieve two purposes. One is to raise extra money for the relief of world hunger. The last couple of years we have cleared well over $10,000 from each workshop. The second purpose is to make available to church leaders from our part of the country a training event that otherwise might not be available to them."

Foundations and Denominational Grants

The most competitive of the twenty-seven supplemental sources of congregational income described in this chapter is the foundation grant. This method for expanding the financial base of the congregation came into popularity in the 1960s when thousands of churches, both Protestant and Catholic, received grants from foundations for a huge variety of programs. These ranged from the financing of community surveys to experimental ministries to private academies to community-action efforts to helping disadvantaged children. As the years passed, the competition for foundation grants increased and the variety of projects multiplied to include feeding the hungry, caring for the victims of AIDS, sheltering the homeless, helping abused women and children, providing adult day care, and scores of other social welfare programs.

For many years a growing variety of federal and state agencies also made direct grants to churches or offered guaranteed loans or subsidized social action and social welfare programs including the delivery of health care services, help to undocumented aliens in securing the proper papers, care for pregnant teenage girls, aid to runaway children, and counseling services.

In addition, several denominations now offer modest grants to assist congregations seeking to make their facilities more accessible to the handicapped or to initiate new ministries or to relocate the meetingplace or to enable a small congregation to enjoy the services of a full-time resident pastor or to fulfill other needs that cannot be financed locally.

Affluence, denominational mergers, guilt, population shifts, and other factors have encouraged this trend. Today the number of available grants is beyond counting, and the range of possibilities is ever expanding, but the possibilities vary greatly from one denomination to another and from one place to another. The only constant is that the competition is increasing faster than the expansion of the resources.

Those who oppose auctions, bazaars, garage sales, and other money-raising activities on the grounds they undercut the health and vitality of a congregation may raise even more strenuous objections to grants and subsidies. Experience suggests denominational grants to subsidize the salary of the underemployed pastor often create a sense of dependency and erode the vitality and initiative of the congregation. In addition, this practice can encourage poor work habits as the pastor learns how to take eight hours to complete four hours of work.

By contrast, reliance on the Lord's acre, auctions, bazaars, and other money-raising activities, rather than seeking outside grants and subsidies, may encourage a better sense of stewardship, strengthen self-dependence, spark initiative, and reward creativity as well as provide entry points for newcomers to become involved.

Increase Attendance

While it does not fit as neatly into the category of supplemental sources as do most of the alternatives offered in this chapter, the closest to a guaranteed means for expanding the financial base is to focus on increasing worship attendance.

The best single predictor of the amount of money contributed in a year is not the size of the membership or the amount of the indebtedness or the income level of the members. The most reliable indicator is the average attendance at worship on the Sabbath. Close behind are the denominational affiliation, or absence of affiliation, the ratio of worship attendance to membership, the rural-urban-suburban division and whether or not that congregation is served by a full-time resident pastor who does not have any other employment and does not serve any other church.

At the top of that list in reliability as a predictor, however, is the average attendance at worship. The higher that average, the higher the per-attender-average giving. For example, in 1989 it was not unusual to find congregations averaging 25 to 35 at worship in which the total member giving for the previous year was $500 (or less) times that average attendance. It also was easy in 1989 to find congregations averaging 300 to 700 at worship in which member giving was equivalent to $1,000 (or more) times the average attendance at worship. The basic generalization is that as worship attendance increases, the level of giving *per attender* also climbs. By contrast, it is not unusual for worship attendance to decline during the same years the reported membership is climbing. Likewise it is not unusual for *per member* giving to decrease concurrently with an increase in the reported membership figure.

High on this list of possibilities for expanding the financial base of your congregation should be the goal of increasing worship attendance. This may be in the form of increasing the frequency of attendance of the current members or increasing the number of people who attend at least once in a typical month or both. Those are the only two ways of increasing worship attendance.

Which of these alternative for expanding the financial base of your congregation has the most appeal to you? How will you seek to implement that concept?

CHAPTER EIGHT

What Do You Do Next?

A reasonable assumption is that anyone who read through the first seven chapters of this book is interested in expanding the financial base of a particular congregation. What do you do next? It is impossible to suggest one strategy or course of action that will be appropriate for every situation, so it may be useful to offer a dozen alternatives.

1. Do nothing. This may be the easiest response.

2. Pass this book on to a member of the finance commission or stewardship committee in your church.

3. Pick out one of the forty-four alternatives offered here and seek to encourage your congregation to implement it.

4. Assume many will disagree with your recommendation, so select two or three of what you believe might be the most appropriate alternatives and offer choices to the policy-makers.

5. Ask for the selection of an ad hoc study committee to examine various alternatives and submit a recommended course of action. This

Of course, we could always do nothing!

FRIAR TUCK

I ALWAYS WANTED TO BE IN PICTURES!

Build informal meetings around cartoon transparencies!

—FRIAR TUCK

assumes that substantial discontent with the financial base of your congregation already exists.

6. If you are the only person in that congregation who is discontented with the level of financial support, ask for selection of an ad hoc study committee to study the financial needs of your congregation over the next five years. That can be one means of broadening the base of discontent with the status quo. This process can be improved by identifying two congregations that (a) five years ago resembled your congregation as it is today and (b) today resembles your vision of what this congregation could be five years hence. Schedule a visit by that special study committee to each of these two congregations. Visit them on their turf. Ask what they did and how they accomplished it.

7. Schedule a congregational meeting for some evening, make transparencies of the Friar Tuck cartoons in this book and plan a presentation built around those cartoons on what could happen. Design this to be an informational meeting on alternatives. Follow the presentation with a group discussion on what those present see as the logical next step.

8. Run a short item in your church's newsletter, again using the Friar Tuck cartoons, to lift up one alternative. Limit this to one alternative and one cartoon per issue.

9. Ask your finance commission or stewardship committee to appoint a special subcommittee to examine alternatives. This may not be as creative as suggestion five, but may be easier to accomplish.

Warning: Others may try to shoot more than your ideas full of holes!

—FRIAR TUCK

10. Propose a course of action, such as a new ministry or expansion of the present program or the addition of a staff member or renovation of the building or the purchase of additional land that will require more money. Choose the appropriate alternatives from the material presented in this book as the recommended means for financing this new need.

11. Create a self-appointed ad hoc group of three to seven people, including one minister, who will meet at least three times over the space of two months to study this book and prepare recommendations to be submitted to the appropriate group for consideration. The advantage of this approach is you can control who will be a member of this ad hoc group. The disadvantage is it does not have any official status, but that may be irrelevant if the membership of that ad hoc group includes two or three highly influential and widely respected individuals.

12. Appoint yourself as the leader of an unofficial one-person crusade. Recognize that persistence often wins in the long run. Accept the fact that you may be rebuffed, ignored, defeated, snubbed, rejected, van-

Note: It is difficult, if not very rare, to lose forty-four consecutive battles!

—FRIAR TUCK

quished, crushed, outvoted, beaten, scorned, and discredited in your first forty-three attempts to expand the financial base of your congregation. Rest secure in the knowledge that no later than your forty-fourth effort persistence will be rewarded and you will prevail. That is why we offer forty-four ways to expand the financial base of your congregation. It is difficult, and very rare, to lose forty-four consecutive battles!

The Invisible Revolution

This book is directed at those persons concerned with expanding the financial base for a congregation's life, ministry, and outreach. An overlapping group of ecclesiastical leaders, however, face a different set of questions. One reason for this is a radical change in the giving patterns of church members on the North American continent.

For approximately six or seven decades most of the old-line Protestant denominations encouraged individuals and families to contribute directly to the congregation to which they belonged. These churches in turn would allocate part of their total receipts to a variety of denominational agencies, including the regional judicatories, national departments of mission, colleges, theological seminaries, and other organizations.

During the 1950s and early 1960s when the conciliar movement was at its peak, local churches contributed to the support of a ministerial association or council of churches. The regional judicatories would contribute out of their income to the state council of churches and the national agencies would contribute to the support of national and worldwide interchurch agencies. One reason that system became so popular was that it reinforced the goal of a unified budget. Instead of a large number of special appeals from a wide range of causes, every participating congregation could prepare one budget for the year and allocated a portion of the total receipts, typically somewhere between 12 and 20 percent, to denominational, interchurch, and local causes.

This pleased those who supported the dream of "let's ask our people for pledges only once a year and divide what we get equitably among all of the askings." It also was consistent with the goals of those who wanted a unified budget at the regional and national levels of that denomination. The system was consistent with those who favored a "businesslike" and efficient approach to church finances. The basic concept was reinforced by the strong denominational ties of that era. Best of all, it worked.

By the mid-1960s, however, that approach was beginning to be eroded by changes in our society. Inflationary rates of 5 to 14 percent annually undercut the viability of the unified budget. An increasing variety of causes and organizations began to appeal to the various judicatories for funding. The cost, in U.S. dollars, of supporting a missionary for one year tripled or quadrupled as the dollar dropped on the international rates. The generations born after 1940 did not feel the sense of denominational loyalty that motivated their parents. Investigative reporters no longer exempted the churches from public criticism. The stewardship education programs of the 1950s and 1960s turned out to be remarkably effective—and many of the laity concluded that responsible stewardship included making sure one's financial contributions were used for purposes consistent with the donor's values and goals.

The 1960s gave birth to an unprecedented number of parachurch ministries that approached Christians individually for financial support. Most of the television preachers depended on direct financial support from individuals, rather than from churches or denominational agencies. The techniques for direct mail financial appeals emerged and were perfected. Public universities, who once depended on the state legislature for most of their funds, discovered it was possible to raise hundreds of millions of dollars by appealing directly to alumni, corporations, and the general public. The United Presbyterian Church in the late 1960s launched a special $50 million appeal for missions and collected over $70 million. Fifteen years later, after scores of denominational appeals directed at individuals, the Lutheran Church-Missouri Synod set a goal of $40 million in its "Forward in Remembrance" financial campaign and collected over $70 million. Church-related colleges and theological seminaries also scheduled successful multimillion dollar capital funds appeals. Many of these appeals were directed at individuals rather than to the budget committees of local churches.

One of the factors behind the extraordinary success of these financial appeals was the huge increase in personal income after 1950. Another reason was the growing number of church members who insisted on knowing exactly where their contributions would go and how they would be used. Many ecclesiastical leaders deplored this growing emphasis on the right of the donor to designate where those contributions would go, but at the same time utilized the appeal of that concept to raise millions for designated causes.

The past three decades have brought a significant decline in the percentage of congregational expenditures that have been sent to (a) national denominational headquarters, (b) denominationally sponsored missionary endeavors outside of North America, (c) regional and national interchurch agencies, and (d) church-related institutions of higher education.

These same years have brought a sharp increase in the proportion of all funds contributed by North American Christians that go directly from the donor to (a) parachurch organizations, (b) television ministries, (c) institutions of higher education, (d) independent missionaries who seek their own financial support directly from individuals and congregations, (e) non-denominational local social welfare agencies, (f) black colleges, (g) children's homes, (h) the relief of world hunger, (i) retreat centers, (j) health care services, (k) shelter for the homeless, (l) needs of a family in crisis, (m) organization of new congregations, and (n) agencies concerned with the care of the elderly.

Two lessons emerge from an examination of this revolution in giving. The first is the growing number of Christians who will contribute generously to what they are convinced is a worthy cause, but are reluctant to give their money to an organization for unspecified purposes. The second lesson is for those institutions and organizations that once depended largely on congregations and denominational agencies for funding. They appear to be faced with six choices: (a) continue their dependence on these sources of funding and make the necessary cutbacks in program and staffing, (b) place a greater reliance on user fees, (c) build up an endowment fund to finance an increasing part of their future ministry, (d) seek public funding, (e) ask for help from foundations, or (f) appeal directly to individuals for financial support. Some have decided to pursue all six possibilities, but the one most likely to yield substantial funds is the direct appeal to individuals.

That means a new set of rules for expanding the financial base of those religious organizations that once depended largely on congregational support. That also means more competition for the financial contributions of individual Christians. This invisible revolution also has created a new context for expanding the financial base of your congregation. One response to that new context is to offer people a broader range of choices—and that is the purpose of this book.